THE EXPLODING MYSTERY
OF PRAYER

Helen Smith Shoemaker

THE EXPLODING MYSTERY OF PRAYER

A CROSSROAD BOOK
The Seabury Press, New York

1978
The Seabury Press
815 Second Avenue
New York, N.Y. 10017

Printed in the United States of America

Library of Congress Cataloging in Publication Data
Shoemaker, Helen Smith.   The exploding mystery of prayer.
"A Crossroad book."
1. Christian life—Anglican authors. 2. Prayer. I. Title.
BV4501.2.S439   248'.3   77-16143   ISBN 0-8164-2183-8

All quotations from the Bible are from the King James version.

CONTENTS

FOREWORD

THERE are two means of sharing prayer with others. The first, of course, is to pray for them. The benefits of prayer offered for another person may not be consciously realized by that person. Nevertheless, whenever we pray in faith and love for someone by name, they have shared our prayers.

The second means of sharing prayer with others is to share with them faith, understanding and experience through the spoken or written word.

Helen Shoemaker shares her prayers faithfully in this two-fold manner with an innumerable company of people. Because she has daily included in her life the exercise of prayer for specific peoples, needs and causes, and because she has been open to receive from others their prayer sharings both in her writings and speaking, she has much to offer of the power—the mysterious and moving power—of prayer.

Both Helen Shoemaker and her late husband, the Rev. Dr. Samuel Shoemaker, have been blessed with the gift of expressing profound and often remote truths in simple, clear and familiar terms. Following the example of the Lord Jesus Christ to whom they both have dedicated their lives, their understanding of Christian love and faith and prayer is often shared through illustrations, parables and descriptions of the commonplace where people live and move and have their being.

This book illustrates the belief that the mystery and wonder and beauty and power of prayer is in the here and now, where people really live, and thereby or therein is readily available to each and all of us, whatever our state of life may be, in the simplicity of our daily living.

The mystery of prayer, like God with whom prayers communicate, is well expressed in the question: "How can the sublime be so available to the ridiculous?"

There are those who have discovered that this sublime mystery becomes less mysterious through *sharing*. Helen Shoemaker is one of them.

JOHN M. ALLIN
Presiding Bishop
The Episcopal Church

> "But we speak the wisdom of God in a mystery, even the hidden wisdom, which God ordained before the world unto our glory."
>
> I CORINTHIANS 2:7

1 ✤ MYSTERY

PRAYER is a mystery of incalculable power. Like the great mysterious underground river that supplies a city with water as it flows beneath the earth and purifies the water so that the city can drink it, so is prayer a mysterious, underground purifying force that for centuries has flowed secretly and hiddenly and steadily beneath the surface clashes and tensions of world forces. Prayer determines whether light shall overcome darkness, whether goodness shall overcome evil. It explodes like a rocket in the night sky, giving off rainbow showers of sparks.

In this book I am hoping to throw light on the mystery which has baffled men and women for centuries. The mystery of God and prayer. If there is a God, is He an impersonal force, a gray oblong blob, or can He talk to us and we to Him? The Bible says He is personal and He can talk to us and we to Him.

Does He send mysterious gifts and powers and healings and manifestations our way when we cry out to Him?

Does He influence the direction of nations when even a handful of persons seek His help and direction?

Does He show us His will and plan when we ask Him?

I

Does He overcome the demonic influences which constantly seek to upset the balance of nature and society?

Did St. Paul have a mysterious flash of insight when he compared these demonic forces to the principalities, the powers, the rulers of the darkness of this universe, spiritual wickedness in high places?

Does prayer hurl itself against these forces with a power and persistence that is unquenchable and irresistible?

Has this been happening through all the centuries of the life of man and is there the possibility that this great mysterious force, this river that flows so persistently underneath all that goes on in the universe, will one day release the power of God in such almighty brilliance that it will flood the universe and drive out all its impurities?

The universe itself is aflash with mystery. Did it just happen or did a great force called God speak it into being? Some, not knowing how to describe it, talk about the "music of the spheres." Moderns tend to carry our minds into the awe-inspiring contemplation of billions of galaxies and the possibility of mysterious living beings of some kind or other inhabiting stars in those galaxies. Anyone who studies the heavens is over-awed with the wonder of it all. Think of the awe felt by the three kings, astrologers of the ancient world, as they came to worship the new-born King guided by the mysterious star which they had observed in the heavens.

Then there is the mystery of the earth. The Genesis story is a beautiful symbolic description of how the earth came into being. Some scientists have described it as a mighty atomic explosion, others describe it in other ways. That it came into being by the mysterious word of God, there can be no doubt. For instance, as we look at the beauty of the natural world around us, those of us who bow before wonder and mystery can observe sunrises and sunsets, northern lights, the wonder of an evening in the country when the busy world is hushed and the fever of life seems low-key, sleepy birds twittering in the trees before they tuck their heads under their wings for the night, the wind whispering softly and rustling the leaves of the trees, the long, beautiful golden shadows of sunset creeping through the grass and fields and turning the ground in the summer to emerald green as glowworms and fireflies twinkle in the grass. In the winter the fields and woods and city streets turn to rosy halos of color around the lamps and outdoor lights; and in the aqua sky is a tiny sickle moon with the brilliantly flaming ice-white evening star beside it.

I rejoice in the fact that so many young people are deeply concerned with nature and want to keep it beautiful and free and wild. I was brought up in Colorado where the beauty and terror of nature was a flashing thing; the gorgeous outlines of high snow-capped mountains, the wonder of great stands of forest trees, the crystal streams and waterfalls and still dark pools, the amazing color of wild flowers in secret mountain meadows and on the vast prairies, the great blizzards that come in the winter, the crashing, flashing thunderstorms, which we called cloud bursts, flooding the dry creeks and sometimes causing great havoc.

Then there are the frightening manifestations of nature; we are lost in fear and wonder as we observe them—mighty earthquakes, great tidal waves, hurricanes, typhoons, cyclones, tornados, drought and flood—events that caused the ancients to cry out to their gods and often try to placate them with offerings of human lives.

And what of the animals? Interesting that, in the story of Genesis, God created the earth and the stones and plants and trees and rivers and streams in successive acts of creation, and next to last created the animals. We read of them being created two by two so that they will propagate on the earth. Animals of every kind and description to fit every kind of climate: the beautiful, sleek, magnificent animals; the ugly, predatory, lumpy animals. There they all are, each with their ordered life styles, their extraordinary sense of territorial possession, their built-in instinct for the hunt and the kill and survival, their mating habits. And then there are the birds. It is not surprising that in the history of the great religions the angels of God have wings because we have observed through the centuries the beauty of the flying creatures of the earth— the birds, with their ability to fly thousands of miles in migration to their winter haunts and back to their nesting places in the summer in the far north, rarely missing their pin-pointed habitats. How did this all happen? There are beautiful birds, there are ugly birds, there are water birds, there are land birds. Every variety with its own way of life, its own mating habits. I recently read that the Siberian blue geese, 100,000 of them, walk a hundred miles in the late summer until their pinions are strong enough to carry them across the Himalayas where they are in danger of being caught and brought down by the thousands in the terrific air drafts which sweep through these mighty mountains. When these geese are airborne nothing will stop them but the down drafts over the mountains. If any of them falter and come down, then the mate will come down with them and stay with them until they die together. But somehow or other, in spite of their casualties, they get over the mountains to their winter quarters in northern India and then fly back again in summer to northern Siberia for their breeding and nesting.

Finally, we come to the creation of man. The writer of the psalms cries out with mysterious and wonderful insight, "What is man that thou art mindful of him or the son of man that thou visiteth him? Thou hast made him little lower than the angels, thou crownest him with glory and honor, and didst set him over the works of thy hands" (Psalm 8). What a mysterious being is man, the crowning accomplishment of God's creation. There is the mystery of why some men and women are dazzlingly beautiful and others homely and earthy looking; why some men and women seem to be enormously gifted and others hardly gifted at all; why some men and women seem born to rule, others destined to be ruled. That is all beyond our comprehension, hidden in the mystery of the mind of God.

The body of a human being is so exquisitely and sensitively formed that one stands in awe in front of it and understands perfectly well why the Greeks made a cult of the body, made the body beautiful almost an object of worship, so that we see hymns of praise in honor of the body expressed in the great statues of Praxiteles.

What indeed is man that "thou Oh, Lord art mindful of him and the son of man that thou visiteth him?" What an extraordinary mystery that men and women have the capacity to do what they do with their minds and bodies and souls; that they seem created to complement each other; that each has particular qualities that the other does not have which, when they are brought together in the union of marriage for instance, illustrates a whole and fulfilled human being. What heights of genius and creativity we have scaled and to what extraordinary depths of evil we have fallen. What insights into the absolute truth of God and the universe we have been given. What creative good has come to the world through the great geniuses of history—the spiritual geniuses like Mohammed and Buddha and St. Paul; the philosophical geniuses like Socrates and Plato; the musical geniuses like Paderewski and Kreisler and Marian Anderson; the artistic geniuses like Michelangelo and Rembrandt and Leonardo Da Vinci; the scientific geniuses like Galileo and Einstein; the great medical geniuses like Pasteur and the Curies.

At the same time there is the mystery of the dark side of man, just as there is the mystery of the dark side of nature and the dark side of the animal world. One wonders how it happens that at the same time as the great saints, the great purveyors of light and progress, there have appeared on the stage of history great megalomaniac conquerors like Alexander or Genghis Khan or Attila or Napoleon. And why has the modern world been scourged by tyrants like Hitler and Stalin and Mao who, together, are responsible for the deaths of millions?

No wonder that, in some of the most mysterious passages

of the Bible, Jesus talks as much as he does about the conflict between light and darkness, between good and evil, between God and Satan, between creativity and discreativity. No wonder that the history of the world as we know it has been so constantly and continuously drenched with the blood of millions of innocent people and the beauty and art and culture of civilization is destroyed by continual warfare. What is this mysterious violence that seems to be part and parcel of the nature of man and which can only be balanced by the equally mysterious creative forces which God has also planted in the human soul? No wonder it has taken prophets, priests, kings and philosophers, and finally God himself, coming to us to attempt to lighten our darkness and confusion and to give us perspective concerning all these bewildering counterforces in nature and in the world which seem to be held in a state of constant tension, at times permeated with so much light and so much spiritual power that we think our desperate need for peace and happiness will be granted; at other times permeated with so much battle, murder and sudden death that we seem to be victims of the principalities and powers and the rulers of the darkness of the universe.

These are the mysteries we are called upon to contemplate, to see if we can thrust through to the heart of the truths which lie buried in the midst of them all.

Thomas Carlyle said, "Worship is transcendent awe." Dr. C. Fitzsimons Allison, rector of Grace Church in New York City, says, "People around us are hungry for the dimension of mystery." The translation of *mysterion* from the Greek means "revealed secret." The Christian "mystery" is that which has been revealed by God in Jesus Christ.

As we enter into the mysteries—especially the mystery of prayer—that I hope to describe in this small book, we can only fall to our knees in worship before Him our Lord and our God, who alone throws light for us onto the meaning of the mysteries which so confuse and bewilder us poor mortals.

> "In the beginning was the Word and the Word was with God and the Word was God."
>
> ST. JOHN I:I

⚸⚬⚬⚬⚬⚬⚬⚬⚬⚬⚬⚬⚬⚬⚬⚬⚬⚬⚬⚬⚬⚬⚬⚬⚬⚬⚬⚬⚬⚬⚬⚬⚬⚬⚬⚬

2 * THE MYSTERY AND WONDER OF GOD

SOME men describe Him as the great life force, others as the ground of their being. Primitive people worship the sun as God and some people believe that He reveals Himself in the terrifying forces of nature—earthquakes, tidal waves, wind and fire. There are those who see Him as many-faceted, representing the god of thunder or the god of the sea. All of these are perhaps attempts at creating Him in our image rather than letting Him create us in His.

It is also a recognition that He is totally "other," mysterious and, yet, He is a God of self-revelation. The Bible holds for me the supreme description of God, for in it God reveals Himself and speaks to His people. In the very first chapter of Genesis, the inspired writer tells us that "In the beginning God." Out of this statement pours the great drama of His dealings with the human beings which He chose for His purposes.

He reveals Himself to Noah and directs him.

He reveals Himself to Abraham and promises him, "I will

7

make thee a great nation. In thee shall all the families of the earth be blest.''

He reveals Himself to Jacob in the disguise of an angel and calls him "Israel."

He reveals Himself to Joseph disguised in dreams and uses him through His dream power to become Pharaoh's right-hand man.

Later He reveals Himself to Moses disguised as an angel in the burning bush. He speaks to Moses out of the bush and tells Moses that he has been chosen to lead his people Israel out of Egypt. God reveals Himself again with the flaming words, "I AM THAT I AM, I AM HATH SENT ME TO YOU. Say to Israel, the Lord God of your fathers, the God of Abraham, the God of Isaac, the God of Jacob appeared unto me and sent me to rescue you from the king of Egypt. And unto the king of Egypt you shall say, 'The Lord God of the Hebrews hath sent me to you.' "

One of the most startling facts in the Bible is the continuous dialogue between God and man. Many passages open with "and God said unto him," and every one of the great figures of both the Old and the New Testament highlight the conversation between God and man. It begins with Adam and Eve, then Noah and Moses, Joshua and Gideon, Saul and David, all the prophets, Jesus, the disciples, and Paul and John, to name only the greatest. And the psalms are the greatest recorded conversations in history between man and his Creator.

He was a God of terrible justice; He visited great plagues on the Egyptians because Pharaoh would not let His people go.

He revealed Himself as a God of protection and intervention when He appeared as a pillar of fire by night to the fleeing Israelites and a pillar of cloud by day to shield them from the pursuing Egyptians.

He revealed Himself as an intervening God for He opened

the Red Sea so that all 250,000 Israelites with their cattle might pass through and then closed it behind them so that the Egyptians might not follow.

He revealed Himself as a God who loved moral order. During the forty years that the Israelites traveled through the wilderness, He ordered Moses up onto Mt. Sinai, and we are told that "Mt. Sinai was altogether on a smoke because the Lord descended upon it in fire." Moses spoke and God answered him like the voice of a trumpet and gave him the Ten Commandments hewn with fire on two tablets of stone—the greatest moral code ever written.

And so it goes all through the Old Testament, God appearing sometimes disguised as a man, sometimes as an angel, often veiled in mystery but always commanding, rebuking, pleading, promising, leading—through Joshua, Gideon, David, the prophets—the great chosen channels of His ever-living design to redeem the world He had created until He showed Himself in Jesus, God in human flesh, to love and live and die and rise from the dead for us.

Does not God ultimately identify Himself as Jesus and Jesus identify Himself as God when He says, "I and the Father are one. He that hath seen Me hath seen the Father."

Through the whole majestic sweep of the Bible, God is progressively revealing Himself in history, in revelation, in power and in love until finally St. Paul tells us we see, "The light of the knowledge of the Glory of God in the face of Jesus Christ."

"Begotten of His father before all worlds,
God of God, Light of Light, very God of
very God. Begotten not made, being of one
substance with the Father by whom all
things are made."

THE NICENE CREED

3 ✳ THE MYSTERY AND WONDER OF JESUS

THIS person, who is He? Where has He come from?
Where is He now? What does He offer?

We have a mysterious insight into who Jesus is in the great
words of the Nicene Creed when we say, "He is God of
God, Light of Light, Very God of Very God, begotten, not
made, being of one substance with the Father by whom all
things were made."

This description of our Lord is particularly stirring. It was
written at the Council of Nicea, shortly after the accession to
power of Constantine the Great, when a statement of faith
needed desperately to be made. There were two great con-
tending forces in the Christian Church at that time, those who
followed Arius and those who followed Athansius. The
Nicene Creed came out of that historic debate, and it became
the mind of the whole Western Church as to who Jesus was.

The wonder of Jesus is also involved with the way in

which He chose to come into the world—through a woman, the same as every human child. He grew to manhood as every human child does. He permitted Himself to be baptized as good Jews of that day were baptized. But there was a mysterious difference. At His baptism He was acknowledged by God the Father, "This is my beloved Son, hear Him," and Jesus was anointed with the mystery of the Holy Spirit.

At His death He again identified Himself with man and died the worst possible kind of death so that He might identify with the worst possible type of sinner and atone for and redeem us all.

After the resurrection, when Jesus appeared in His supernatural body, He anointed the disciples with His Spirit just as He had been anointed at His baptism. His Holy Spirit flowed through the disciples into the pagan world and established His mysterious body—the Church. We acknowledge this mystery when we sing:

The Church's one foundation is Jesus Christ her Lord;
She is His new creation, By water and the Word;
From Heaven He came and sought her To be His holy bride
With His own blood He bought her, and for her life He died.

To learn about Him further one must study Him in prayer. In the gospel stories of Jesus we are often told that He climbed a mountain to pray. On one such mountain, known to the world as the Mount of Transfiguration, He moved away from the three whom He had chosen to be with Him and knelt in prayer. Before the astonished gaze of Peter, James and John, Jesus' raiment became white and glistening—He reflected the eternal radiance of His Father. This was such an overwhelming experience to His disciples that Peter, in his impulsive fashion, suggested that they build a tabernacle and stay there forever with Jesus basking in His splendor.

Jesus paid no attention to Peter and quickly led them down the mountain. There Jesus is confronted with His other disciples who are trying in vain to help a man who is in despair about his epileptic child. Jesus, having just totally identified with the eternal power and energy of God, challenges the father of the child to renew his faith, and heals the child. The disciples then ask Jesus how He is able to cure the child when they could not. He replies sternly, "This kind only comes out by prayer and fasting," and then makes a stupendous promise about the mysterious power of prayer and fasting, when He says in reply to their question again, "For verily I say unto you, if ye have faith as a grain of mustard seed, ye shall say unto this mountain, remove thence to yonder place and it shall remove; and *nothing shall be impossible to you"* (Matthew 17:20). He doesn't tell them how long He has fasted on the Mount of Transfiguration before the ineffable experience of glory occurs. We understand that there must have been fasting and prayer in connection with it for the super-conscious energy which resulted witnessed to the mysterious truth of this need for self-denial and prayer before this miracle could take place. As Jesus fasted and prayed, so He tells us must we.

The story of St. Francis of Assisi is one aflash with the mystery of fasting and prayer and Jesus.

Francis was kneeling outside his hut. His prayer quivered in the silence of the night, dawn was near. It was bitingly cold, and the stars were shining brightly in the sky. And then, as the first glimmer of light appeared in the dark, what he had lived for all his life happened.

All of a sudden there was a dazzling light. It was as though the heavens were exploding and splashing forth all their glory in millions of waterfalls of colors and stars. And in the center of that bright whirlpool was a core of blinding light that flashed down from the depths of the sky with terrifying speed until suddenly it stopped, motionless and sacred, above a pointed rock in front of St.

Francis. It was a fiery figure with wings, nailed to a cross of fire. Two flaming wings rose straight upward, two others opened out horizontally, and two more covered the figure. And the wounds in the hands and feet and heart were blazing rays of blood. The sparkling features of the Being wore an expression of supernatural beauty and grief. It was the face of Jesus, and He spoke.

Then suddenly streams of fire and blood shot from His wounds and pierced the hands and feet of Francis with nails, and his heart with the stab of a lance. As Francis uttered a mighty shout of joy and pain, the fiery image impressed itself into his body, as into a mirrored reflection of itself, with all its love, its beauty and its grief. And it vanished within him. Another cry pierced the air. Then with nails and wounds through his body, and with his soul and spirit aflame, St. Francis sank down unconscious in his blood.*

Jesus' appearances to men and women have occurred again and again throughout history and are even occurring in the United States of America. Very recently, on Holy Thursday evening, an unknown elderly priest in an unknown small church, in an almost unknown small coal town in the United States was celebrating Holy Communion in remembrance of the Last Supper. This priest, who had gone into the ministry late in life, celebrated communion every day in his parish of one hundred people. All one hundred of them, in groups of twenty-five, attended the Holy Communion every day of the week. After the priest had celebrated the sacrament and placed the veil on the chalice, he suddenly saw the face of the Christ clearly outlined inside the veil, wearing the crown of thorns. He said nothing about this as he was the kind of person who did not wish publicity and did not believe in sensationalism. He thought perhaps that this was a visitation of encouragement to himself. On Easter Sunday the Holy Communion was celebrated both at the early service and at one or two other services during the day. The image had disap-

*Felix Timmermans, *The Perfect Joy of St. Francis* (Garden City, New York: Doubleday/Image, 1974).

peared from the veil on the chalice. Two weeks later when the reserve sacrament had been removed to the tabernacle with a veil over it, a young mother was praying before the tabernacle with her little girl beside her. Suddenly the little girl poked her mother and said, "Mother, Mother, look. I see God up on the altar. Look. Look." The Mother looked and there was the same wonderful, compassionate face outlined inside of the veil. Two weeks after that, a visiting priest took over a service of Holy Communion with the laying on of hands and the anointing of oil. A woman came to the service with a blue child who was dying. As she came forward for the sacrament and the laying on of hands, the child suddenly became pink and rosy and seemed completely healed, much to the astonishment of the visiting priest. That day the face reappeared on the veil of the chalice. The priest told his bishop of this occurrence and the bishop, being a great man of God, came himself to see what had happened. He also saw the dim outline of his Lord's face. And he felt in this small church a holiness and a quiet and a sense of beauty and power that he had not felt for a long time. The bishop wrote his people a letter about it in his diocesan newspaper. The result of this and the fact that people began to talk soon called the matter to the attention of the press. Since Holy Thursday night when our Lord's face first appeared on the veil of the chalice, 100,000 hungry, needy and hopeful people have come to that small church in that small coal town. Some have seen the face, some have not seen the face, some have received a blessing, some have not received a blessing. A dear friend of mine, the wife of a priest, went with her husband to visit this small church, not because she was curious, but because she was devout. She felt a sense of mystery and wonder as she entered the church. She fell on her knees and prayed ardently that she might see the face. She was at a point in her life when she needed reassurance. As hard as she looked, she saw nothing. She finally said, "Lord, take away this desire of mine to see you if you don't want me to see you, and please keep my faith and hope as strong as ever, and please above all things hear my prayer for these members of my family." She then named the various members of her family who needed prayers at that time. She looked up from her prayers after ten or fifteen minutes and there, clearly outlined on the veil like a faded photograph, was the beautiful head of our Lord. His eyes were looking right at her. She was overcome with awe and the mystery of it. As she went out of the church she wanted to reassure herself that she had really truly seen Him, so she looked back and the face was still there looking at her.

And finally I, myself, felt irresistibly drawn to Shamokin. I went with Donald Hultstrand, the new Executive Director of the Anglican Fellowship of Prayer. It was a long way— three hours from Baltimore—to match a great longing. I met Don in Lancaster, Pennsylvania, where he lives, and we drove up together. We both felt like the two men from Greece who came to find Jesus just before His Passion. They looked for Him everywhere and finally found Him in Jerusalem. They timidly approached one of His disciples and asked, "Sir, we would see Jesus," and the disciples took them to see Jesus. We all know the outcome of that meeting.

The spiritual adventure of our Shamokin pilgrimage is indescribable. After driving through glorious country we came to this small and yet rather charming, typically American coal town set in the Pennsylvania hills. All the streets seemed to be up and down. All the houses seemed to be up and down, with many stairs leading to houses above other houses. We found our church, a small Pennsylvania stone church of the last century with wood beams, whitewashed walls, mahogany pews and not very beautiful Victorian stained glass (although over the altar there was a quite beautiful window with a flaming angel standing in the middle of it). On the altar were many flowers, many candlesticks, and in the middle

of the altar the ciborium covered with a very heavy white brocaded veil. On top of the veil was a small cross. There was
a litany desk at the foot of the chancel steps and many ranks
of votive candles, mostly lit and flickering everywhere around
the chancel. We kneeled down in the third pew from the
front. It was very quiet, with few people, and as Don kneeled
he saw the face clearly and immediately. His daughter Kathy
and I did not see anything at all. It looked like a brocaded
white shroud with no sign of anything on it. So I said to
myself what my friend had said to herself: "Well, Jesus, I
want to see you more clearly, I could not love you more
dearly, I don't think, and I could not want to follow you
more nearly, but if you don't want to show yourself to me,
that's all right, too. I will say the prayers that I came here to
say. I will light the candles that I came here to light, and I
will go away rejoicing in the Spirit because this has the feel
of a holy place." So I bowed my head. I spent fifteen minutes in my intercessions and when I looked up there were two
long narrow streaks of shadow on the front of the veil, and
inside there began to appear the face of Jesus, faintly at first,
beginning with the brow, two deep hollows where the eyes
were, a long slim nose, what looked like a long, flowing, fair
beard. The two dark shadows on the veil turned into long
straight dark hair. I felt I simply had to go kneel at the litany
desk, and as I kneeled there the face became clearer and
clearer. I saw, although it was rather faint, a rounded chin
with a beard and the faint outlines of a mustache. I
couldn't see much of His mouth, but I saw the lines on either
side of His nose, and there seemed to be a beautiful strong
neck. The whole outline was brilliantly white, with the two
long dark shadows of hair on either side of a long narrow
face. It looked like a beautiful face in marble, strong, yet luminous, and at the same time shadowed. I couldn't take my
eyes away from it. He was there, no question. I went back to
the pew and Don made a drawing for me of what he had

seen, and it was the same face. As we went out, we met a wonderful little Greek Orthodox woman who had more or less adopted the church and who saw other images on the walls—a kneeling figure which she pointed out to us above the second station of the cross, the figure which she thought was Mary on the wall to the right hand side of the chancel, a figure of a beautiful rather faintly luminous cross further down on that wall.

We found an Italian restaurant and had lunch, and the propriotress, a Roman Catholic, filled us in with all kinds of observations on what the face in the veil had meant to the little town, and how much she felt the little town needed it because, she said, "You know the Mafia has gotten control of all the pizza parlors here and kids go and get all kinds of dreadful dope. This spring, before the face appeared on the veil, there was a very vicious teen-age murder, and two young boys filled with dope took two young girls up on the mountain, beat them to death and poured lye on their bodies, set them on fire and buried them. Now you know this town needed Jesus so badly that He came, and yet a lot of ministers here believe that Father Knutti is just using this to exploit his church." Said the Italian woman with her eyes flashing, "I don't believe for one minute he's doing this. He's a very holy man." We agreed with her whole heartedly, and left with our hearts strangely warmed.

Amazing that the little prayer group which meets regularly with Fr. Knutti had prayed for some time that something would happen through that little church which would bring new hope to a troubled world.

What does this say to us, a skeptical, modern, rather pragmatic, cynical, yet enormously spiritually hungry people? Does it say to us perhaps that our Lord has His own way of coming to us in our need? He chooses His own place, He chooses His own time. It is usually a humble place and an unexpected time, but it is always mysterious and wonderful.

While deep in prayer, a well known Presbyterian surgeon, past president of the American Surgical Association, had a vision of death and Jesus in the midst.

The instant I left this world my first sensation was that of being devoid of a material body. The mask of flesh had vanished. I was free from the constraints of an earthly existence; free from the illusion of time. The essential self lay bare. A realization of weightlessness and transparency dawned upon me. The transparency was of a kind that every thought was visible.

This awakening gave way to the consciousness of an aura of peace, the ultimate peace. I was in a universe of peace; peace suffused with joy, an infinite joy, the joy of creation which caused the morning stars to sing together. An ocean of joy bathed my whole being. The joy of redeeming grace welled up within me.

I was aware, too, of a Presence. The Presence was so intensely real, so immediate, that all else faded into oblivion. The Presence was one of measureless might and the overflowing grace were coinherent in the supernal glory of the Presence. Before this infinite Good I was bowed in awesome adoration.

A flood of glory filled my once transparent self, filled me with all the fullness of God and clothed me with a celestial body, the transcendent expression of my earthly frame. The ineffable glory, so freely given wrought a oneness with the Presence and I knew that the Son's affirmation while on earth had been fulfilled.*

The insight of the writer of the Epistle to the Hebrews tells us, "Who being the brightness of His glory, and the express image of His person, and upholding all things by the word of His power, when He had by Himself purged our sins, sat down on the right hand of the Majesty on High" (Hebrews 1:3).

Jesus' most mysterious claim as to who He was comes to us out of St. John's Gospel when He says to Martha, the sis-

* Warfield Firor, "Jesus Is Praying for Us," prepared for The Anglican Fellowship of Prayer.

ter of Lazarus, "I am the resurrection and the Life, He that believeth in me, though he were dead, yet shall he live, and He that liveth and believeth in me shall never die" (St. John 11:25,26).

So that is who He is and that is what He offers—Himself. His many-faceted self, totally identified with our sinful suffering selves and at the same time totally one with God, the giver of resurrected life.

"Greater love hath no man than this, that a man lay down his life for his friend."

ST. JOHN 15:13

✻✼✼✼✼✼✼✼✼✼✼✼✼✼✼✼✼✼✼✼✼✼✼✼✼✼✼✼✼✼✼

4 ✻ THE MYSTERY OF JESUS' SELF-GIVING FOR US

THE Epistle to the Hebrews is pitched to the understanding of the Hebrew congregation who had, in their historic and theological background, a built-in comprehension of the importance of symbolic liturgical worship. The center was the temple with its Holy of Holies where the Ark of the Covenant stood, guarded by the golden cherubim and in the midst God, the "Shekinah," the all powerful, was believed to be present. Into this Holy of Holies the high priest was enjoined to go once a year to sacrifice an unblemished lamb for the sins that the people of God had committed during the year, that their sins might be atoned for.

Why must the lamb be unblemished and why must it go willingly to its death? Because God decreed through Moses that only a creature totally pure and willing could be sacrificed for sin.

The writer of Hebrews takes this wonder-inspiring ancient liturgy and carries us way beyond the sacrifices of the high priest chosen by the people, to the High Priest chosen by God Himself, to enter into the Holy of Holies; once and for all

and forever, to sacrifice His own Body and Blood, the pure
unblemished lamb of God, for the sins of everyone everywhere for evermore. We are carried into realms of ecstasy as
we contemplate this self-oblation of our Lord the great High
Priest Himself, the lamb without blemish, who promises us
in shining words that, because He has done this, "He is able
to save to the uttermost those that come unto God by Him,
seeing that He ever liveth to make intercession for us" (Hebrews). In other words, as He prays eternally for us He
releases God's super-conscious energies and powers to us-
ward.

There is a marvelous verse which has been deleted from
the great hymn, "When I Survey the Wondrous Cross":

His dying crimson like robe
Flows o'er his body on the tree
Then I am dead to all the world,
And all the world is dead to me.

That is why a basic emphasis of the faith of all Christians
is that we have been washed in the blood of the lamb: the
mysterious lamb of God who went voluntarily to His death
for us on a cross where God's necessary justice was over-
ruled by His amazing love.

In his marvelous little book, *The Power of the Blood of
Jesus,* Dr. Andrew Murray says of this mighty passage in
Hebrews:

For victory over sin and the deliverance of the sinner, God has
no other means or thought than "The Blood of Christ."
Yes, it is indeed something that surpasses all understanding.
. . . The blood of Jesus is the greatest mystery of eternity, the
deepest mystery of the divine wisdom. . . . Sacrificial blood
always meant the offering of a life. The Israelite could not obtain
blood for the pardon of his sin unless the life of something that
belonged to him was offered in sacrifice. The Lord Jesus did not

offer up His own life and shed His blood to spare us from the sacrifice of our lives. No indeed! But to make the sacrifice of our lives possible and desirable.

The hidden value of His blood is the spirit of self-sacrifice, and where the blood really touches the heart, it works out in that heart, a like spirit of self-sacrifice. We learn to give up ourselves and our lives, so as to press into the full power of that new life which the blood has provided.*

The heart of Christianity is the blood of Jesus. The blood from His nail-pierced hands is for you and me; the blood from His nail-pierced feet is for you and me; the blood from His spear-pierced heart is for you and me. His body and blood which He gave up to death for us is still our strength and our life as we receive His spiritual body and blood in the Eucharist. And this is offered eternally with His prayers for us.

As Jonathan clothed David with all his princely apparel because his soul clove to him, so Jesus clothes us with all His power and love and peace and joy and insight and wisdom because His soul cleaves to ours. And we love Him because He has always been loving us and always will for ever and ever and ever. Amen.

He pours His body and blood over us; He wraps us in the mantle of His prayers. Who then can separate us from the love of God which is in Christ Jesus our Lord. He has bought us with His own blood so that we may forever live and die free, free, free—HALLELUJAH!

> *If we have never sought, we seek Thee now;*
>   *Thine eyes burn through the dark, our only stars;*
> *We must have sight of thorn-pricks on Thy brow,*
>   *We must have Thee, O Jesus of the Scars.*

* Andrew Murray, *The Power of the Blood of Jesus* (Old Tappan, N.J.: Fleming Revell, 1974).

The heavens frighten us; they are too calm;
In all the universe we have no place.
Our wounds are hurting us; where is the balm?
Lord Jesus, by Thy Scars, we claim Thy grace.

If, when the doors are shut, Thou drawest near,
Only reveal those hands, that side of Thine;
We know to-day what wounds are, have no fear
Show us Thy Scars, we know the countersign.

The other gods were strong; but Thou wast weak;
They rode, but Thou didst stumble to a throne;
But to our wounds only God's wounds can speak,
*And not a god has wounds, but Thou alone.**

---

* William Temple, *Readings in St. John's Gospel* (London: Macmillan, 1950).

"For whosoever will save his life shall lose it: and whosoever will lose his life for my sake shall find it."

ST. MATTHEW 16:25

xᐩᐩᐩᐩᐩᐩᐩᐩᐩᐩᐩᐩᐩᐩᐩᐩᐩᐩᐩᐩᐩᐩᐩᐩᐩᐩᐩᐩᐩᐩᐩᐩx

5 ✳ THE MYSTERY OF OUR SELF-GIVING FOR OTHERS

WHY is it that, as we read the lives of the saints, we see that a mysterious link is binding them together? The link is self-giving and prayer.

We Americans recoil from the idea of denying ourselves anything. We want to be warm, live in comfortable houses, eat well, give our children every advantage in attractive neighborhoods and schools, enjoy status, social position, acceptance. This is all very human and very natural and often very self-indulgent. And yet around us whirls a world full of tumult, hunger, disease, poverty, hatred, division, evil of all kinds. And so while we recoil from self-giving and prayer, our consciences are pricked with anger toward injustice and compassion toward those who are suffering from famine, hunger, earthquake, oppression, disease, the infinite varieties of human grief.

Indignation over oppression and compassion for suffering are Christian virtures because our small indignations over injustice and oppression are a reflection of *His* mighty indignation, and our small compassions are a reflection of *His* eternal compassion for suffering human beings.

But what can we do about it? We can deny ourselves and fast and pray.

Perhaps we cannot all be like St. Francis who embraced and cared for lepers, who gave away all his worldly goods to feed the poor, who endured cold and hunger and extreme poverty, who fasted and prayed constantly, and who, because of his self-imposed asceticism, suffered severe bodily illness and yet could write the hymn to the sun, the St. Francis prayer, heal the sick and receive the stigmata.

Elizabeth Ann Bayley Seton, recently canonized by the Roman Catholic Church, is a mysterious modern example of self-denial, love and prayer. Here was a privileged and beautiful young widow who could easily have remarried, to her friend Antonio Felicci; and yet God had laid His hand on her so definitely for His purpose that she and Antonio felt that marriage was not for them; she went obediently, trustingly, and alone to her high destiny. This destiny embraced illness and death at a very young age, as it did for St. Francis, but that was not important to her. Look for a moment at what she accomplished. She founded a great teaching order in the Roman Catholic Church. She is largely responsible for the beginnings of the parochial school system. She miraculously healed people. She was a great mother.

Then there is your modern St. Theresa of Calcutta, a small wrinkled Albanian nun who has prayed and hurled her life after her prayers into the horrible slums of Calcutta where she receives the body and blood of our Lord in the Eucharist daily and then goes out into the streets in His power to rescue the sick and dying and abandoned, the rejects of society, whom nobody wants but Jesus through Mother Theresa and her nuns.

Or consider the moving story told by Charles Colson in *Born Again* of the offer made by three prominent members of the United States Congress, members of his prayer group, to serve out his term in prison for him giving up all their own status and privileges, so that he might be released to minister to his son who needed him.

Or the offer made by a former Christian president of South Korea, imprisoned by the current dictator there along with several other Christian leaders (protesting for human rights), to suffer actual execution in the Christians' place so that they might go free.

Recall the thousands of great saints through the 2,000 years of Christian history who have withdrawn into desert places or monasteries to fast and pray daily for the needs and the evils and the suffering of the world.

With these examples of self-giving and fasting and prayer before us, is it out of order to ask Jesus, "What do you want me to do, or pray, or give, so that I can obey your great commandment to love my neighbor as myself today? Is it my money you want or my time for someone in need? Do you want me to fast and pray for friends in need or situations in need?"

One friend of mine visits prisoners weekly in a county jail. Here is a letter she has just written to me.

Dear Helen,

I am sure the Lord would like you to know, that you were the instrument He used, to reach me with the message on prayer, that I will use in the County Jail today.

I asked the Lord what message He would have me give these men and women prisoners and here it is.

Prayer is the highest form of thought one can have for another.

Prayer is lovers' conversation, conversation between any two people who love each other; it transcends all human dimensions.

When you pray for someone you know there is nothing you can give, nothing you can say, and nothing you could do that would be of greater value.

Therefore anyone with any time to spend can be an intercessory prayer partner for anyone they love or anyone they know of that has a need. The time that is served in this way will fill the emptiness and loneliness of the heart with more peace, love and joy than any other thing could.

Frankie

Perhaps you are saying to yourself at this point: "But these people are special, specially chosen by God for some great work, and I'm nobody. I'm just an old lonely widow, or a teenager, or a mere housewife, or a day laborer, or a welfare mother, or a small businessman. There's nothing special about me and God would never pick me out to do a great work of prayer or service." How do you know? Each of us is precious in His sight and maybe you are the only one whom He wants to use in a certain work of self-giving love, self-giving prayer, self-giving service to someone or some cause that needs you. Dr. Harry Emerson Fosdick tells us of the power of this self-denying love and prayer in describing the prayer of a mother for a wayward child.

No explanation, however reasonable, can do justice to the experience of vicarious praying. To feel that, we must turn to life. When a mother prays for her wayward son, no words can make clear the vivid reality of her supplications. Her love pours itself out in insistent demand that her boy must not be lost. She is sure of his value, with which no outward thing is worthy to be compared, and of his possibilities which no sin of his can ever make her doubt. She will not give him up. She follows him through his abandonment down to the gates of death; and if she loses him through death into the mystery beyond, she still prays on in secret, with intercession which she may not dare to utter, that wherever in the moral universe he may be, God will reclaim him. As one considers such an experience of vicarious praying, he sees that it is not merely resignation to the will of God; it is urgent assertion of a great desire. She does not really think that she is persuading God to be good to her son, for the courage in her prayer is due to her certain faith that God also must wish that boy to be recovered from his sin. She rather is taking on her heart the same burden that God has on his; is joining her demand with the divine desire. In this system of personal life which makes up the moral universe, she is taking her place alongside God in an urgent, creative outpouring of sacrificial love.

Now, this mother does not know and cannot know just what she is accomplishing by her prayers. But we know that such mothers save their sons when all others fail. The mystery of prayer's projectile force is great, but the certainty of such prayer's influence, one way or another, in working redemption for needy lives is greater still. It may be . . . that God has so ordained the laws of human interrelationship that we can help one another not alone by our deeds but also directly by our thoughts, and that earnest prayer may be the exercise of this power in its highest terms. But whether that mother has ever argued out the theory or not, she still prays on. Her intercession is the utterance of her life; it is love on its knees.*

It is also so mysterious, all we need is to be ready. Are you? am I? He needs us all. He wants us all. He will use us all.

* Harry Emerson Fosdick, *The Meaning of Prayer* (Folcroft, Pa.: Folcraft Library Editions, 1915).

"Verily, verily I say unto thee, except a man be born again, he cannot see the kingdom of God."

ST. JOHN 3:3

6 * THE MYSTERY OF A CHANGED LIFE

JESUS challenges and encourages us to give ourselves in the same complete and obedient fashion as He did so that He can release through us the little daily energies, the little daily graces, the little daily self-givings of which we are capable. He formed us into different families, into different races. He endowed us with different gifts, different opportunities, which He is asking us to present to Him so that He may infuse them with His own eternal power. All these joined to Him release His ultimate creative energies into the world.

Commitment to Jesus Christ is not a one-for-all event. It is the beginning of one's spiritual pilgrimage of discipleship. Those who are disciples of Christ face continual turning points which offer new experiences rooted in being "born anew to a living hope." We never move beyond the need to hear the renewing call to "repent and believe in the gospel" in order to live more obediently to the word of the Lord in every area of life.

For some this being "born again" is a sudden overwhelming experience. For others, especially those brought up in the Church, it is a gradual step-by-step obeying and praying which brings a growing consciousness of who He is and what He is offering to us and asking of us. One thing we all discover is the truth of His great saying, "He that seeketh to save his life shall lose it and he that loseth his life for my sake and the gospels the same shall save it."

Jesus said, "I can of mine own self do nothing, as I hear I judge; for I came down from heaven not to do mine own will but what I see the Father do . . . for the Father loveth the Son, and showeth Him all things that Himself doeth." Jesus constantly refers to having been sent and telling and doing for us what He has been told to do. Then He says, "When the Holy Spirit comes He will guide you into all truth. He shall take of mine and show it unto you." So, we are to listen as He listened, and then we shall know as He knew, and do as He did.

Albert Schweitzer said:

We do not discover Him; He discovers Himself to us. He comes to us as One unknown, without a name, as of old, by the lake-side, He came to those men who knew Him not. He speaks to us the same word: "Follow thou me!" and sets us to the tasks which He has to fulfill for our time. He commands. And to those who obey Him, whether they be wise or simple, He will reveal Himself in the toils, the conflicts, the sufferings which they shall pass through in His fellowship, and as an ineffable mystery, they shall learn in their own experience Who He Is.*

I have been taught to listen since the beginning of my Christian experience. A wise Christian friend once said to me, "God has a plan, you have a part, find it, follow it. You have two ears and one mouth. Why don't you listen twice as

---

* Albert Schweitzer, "Step by Step Quest of the Historical Jesus" (*The Living Church*, December 19, 1976).

much as you talk?'' What a tingling sense of adventure this
has given me about life; throughout the ups and the downs,
the sorrows and the joys, the failures and the successes, there
has run a secret confidence like a golden thread.

Even before my Christian experience, God was gently
nudging me along. I lived in a college town, and many un-
dergraduates spent long hours in our house. One young man
was outstanding. There was a quiet confidence and authority
about him that intrigued me. So one day I asked him what he
had that I didn't have and he quietly told me that he had
found God. I asked him how and he said, ''I took hold of
Him by the handle of my sins.'' To which I replied scorn-
fully, ''I don't believe in sin, what is it anyway?'' He then
informed me that sin is anything that stands between you and
other people or any habit or thought that you can't control. I
immediately thought of all the people I was mad at or jealous
of or who I put down in my mind. I thought of self-pity and
inferiority and envy and pride. So these were sins, were
they?

Shortly after this conversation he led me to a drab little
conference center in a drab little town. I'd never been to a
religious conference and it sounded dull. When we got there
this friend asked me point blank if I would dare to give as
much of myself as I knew to as much of God as I understood,
and I said, ''You mean forever?'' He answered, ''Yes.'' And
I said, ''But what if He asks me to live like St. Francis or
someone like that?'' He replied, ''What if He does? Would
you be willing to do whatever He might ask you for the rest
of your life? Would you like to get free of all those hangups
we've talked about?'' After a long frightening battle with
myself, I said ''Yes!'' I knew many of my friends and family
would think I was crazy or a fanatic. I knew that I might be
asked to change my whole life style, but I said ''Yes,'' and a
mysterious ecstasy flooded my whole being, the afterglow of
which has stayed with me throughout my life. At that point I

knew that the great God, my Creator, had claimed me for His purposes, and that step by step He would unfold them to me. I was an average upper middleclass girl with the social morés of the times, a high school education, plenty of relational hangups, and a interest in art and marriage. I had no formal experience with the Church.

After my conversion experience, my Christian nurture started in small group fellowship and prayer. Four years later, I married a priest of the Church. I had had no experience with death, but a year later I faced the possibility of my own death at the time of the birth of my first child. I had no knowledge of what was demanded of a clergy wife, but I was a clergy wife for thirty-three years, involved in all the challenge and adventure of it. I was called upon to raise two daughters under the public scrutiny of two large congregations. I was plunged into all the intricacies of churchmanship and Christian service and organizational responsibility, and I was led to listen and to fast and to pray over and over and over, because without it I had not the least capacity to cope with it all; but in the mysterious fellowship of prayer and public worship, the rough places were smoothed out and the dark places were lighted, and when I fell down, oh so often, He picked me up and dusted me off and showed me what to do next. It has all been unfolding like a tapestry through the fifty years of life with Him, my never-failing, wonderful friend, Jesus Christ.

Recently He has given me a new joy. Before my conversion experience at the age of 25, I had been deeply interested in the visual arts, and for four or five years had studied sculpture with various excellent teachers in New York. At the time of my marriage, it came to me to give this talent to God along with the rest of me. At the time He did not give it back. It was a complete relinquishment. Some people might say it was a false relinquishment. I could not have married the man I married and pursued the joint ministry with him that I enjoyed if I had determined that I had to be a sculptress as well. It came to me very strongly that I could trust God to use any gifts He had given me, whether they issued in sculpture or whether they issued in other things. My creative gift issued in speaking and writing, in a rich family life and service in the Church, and I was fully satisfied with it for many, many years. It wouldn't have been possible to pursue sculpture because sculpture requires a great deal of time alone, which I did not have during our entire marriage. So it was a tremendous surprise and something of a shock to me when the Holy Spirit said to me recently, "You trained many years ago to be a sculptress. I asked you to give it up. I now want to give it back to you. You can still do it. I want you to do something special for me. I want you to sculpt each of the four archangels. Don't worry. You will know how to do it."

So, in excited obedience, I picked up my modeling tools again. I have sculpted the four archangels. It is a beautiful and mysterious use of a gift that was given in my youth and is being given back to me so that I may praise God with it in my old age. I have asked myself why I have been led to sculpt angels. It began in Pittsburgh when our bishop came to celebrate the Eucharist in our church one Sunday morning. When he said the beautiful spine tingling phrase in the Sanctus of the Episcopal communion service—"with angels and archangels and all the company of heaven, we laud and praise thy glorious name"—he paused at the words "angels and archangels" and, for the first time in my Christian pilgrimage, I became aware that here, near us, were mysterious winged beings of great power about whom I knew very little.

Why have I been led to sculpt angels? Why has Billy Graham been led to write about them? Perhaps the angels want us to draw attention to the fact that they are brooding over our world, guarding and protecting us against the world, the flesh and the devil—the armies of light arrayed against the armies of darkness, the messengers and servants of God.

It is all very mysterious and exciting to me, and it has come about as I have listened to the Holy Spirit.

As a matter of fact, why did He change me in the first place? But when I yielded myself to Him, He did, and I've never regretted it.

Wherever you are, however humble your circumstances, you can join the millions of us who are experiencing the mysterious wonder and adventure of a life under His direction. Are you bold enough to try it? If you do you will be richly blessed and used by our living Lord in ways past your imagining. The ribbon of your life will thread its way in and through suffering, anguish, depression, misunderstanding, hostility, but also through the miracle of joyous surprise and comfort and grace, because He is in the midst of it all with you.

For me, the last verse in Hymn 554 of the Episcopal Hymn Book says it all:

Lead on, O King eternal:
We follow, not with fears;
For gladness breaks like morning
Where'er Thy face appears.
Thy cross is lifted o'er us;
We journey in its light:
The crown awaits the conquest;
Lead on, O God of might!

"Know ye not that ye are the temple of God, and that the Spirit of God dwelleth in you."

I CORINTHIANS 3:16

7 * THE MYSTERY OF THE BODY AS THE TEMPLE OF THE HOLY SPIRIT

ONE of the world's great questions, one which St. Paul posed to the first converts to the Christian faith, is "Do you know that your body is the temple of the Holy Spirit?" He was preaching the Gospel of the Good News of Jesus Christ and His resurrection to a pagan society which was committed to all kinds of erotic and pornographic defilements of the body; he was crying out to this society that these bodies which God had created in His love were so precious to Him that they could become pure temples of His living spirit. He held out to them the glory of what the living spirit of Christ could do with a person who gave his body to this mystery.

There are a number of ways in which we defile the body. One of them is to eat too much or to eat the wrong kinds of food. It is interesting that some young people today are going quite passionately back to the whole idea of eating good, organically grown foods.

We also drink too much. America has become a hard-drinking country, and we all know the terrible toll alcoholism takes on the human body. Here is the diagnosis of the effect of alcohol given me by a member of Alcoholics Anonymous: the alcoholic at first is hail-fellow-well-met. He enjoys crowds and cocktail parties. Then a gradual metamorphosis takes place. He starts to withdraw from his friends, his church, his family, his community. He feels terribly alone and thinks no one else has his problem. He thinks that he'll wake up one day and everything will be okay. He starts to feel unloved and unwanted. He may become very sullen and withdrawn, or he may become belligerent and aggressive. Very often he goes on an ego trip. He says to himself, "I can stop any time I want to, I just don't choose to stop now." Or, "I'm only hurting myself." He becomes highly emotional. There is no serenity or peace of mind. He has no tolerance for stress situations. Whenever a stress situation arises he goes on a drunk and becomes highly explosive and volatile. He creates crises as he goes along. He gets out of one but gets into two more, i.e., he spends his paycheck, he doesn't come home, he totals his car, he gets arrested for drunken driving, he loses his driver's license, he gets arrested for driving on a revoked license, and so on. Many alcoholics have black-outs. They are coherent and ambulatory but don't remember what they did. This is brain cell destruction, not amnesia. About this time they start to fall apart physically— high blood pressure, hypertension, diabetes, alcoholic neuritis, ulcers, cirrhosis of the liver. At this point an alcoholic wants only to exist. He lives in misery. His world is a fantasy world, a facade. He loses purpose in life. Goals become nonexistent. Failure becomes his way of life. Call alcholism the great bankrupter. It will reach into every department of a person's life and slowly but surely destroy it. When alcohol is finished with him or her, only his heart will be beating, and that not for long. Again, there are young idealists rebelling against this excess of drinking, trying in their own way to cut out hard liquor.

Another way we neglect our bodies is by not exercising enough. It takes less energy to just sit down in a car and have the car take you to where you want to go than to walk. Again, some of our young people are turning to jogging and push-ups and tennis and yoga as a way to exercise and keep their bodies in good shape.

Then there are those who are "workaholics": people so consumed with ambition to get to the top of the heap or the center of power—whether in church, business, or the state—that they spend little or no time with their families, spend most of their time on planes or at the office, and often drop dead in their early forties. In the last several weeks four young men of my acquaintance have done just that—dropped dead before their time.

And above all, we've gone overboard on permissive sex. The number of books that are written about sex in its various and sundry forms are legion; they tell how to develop sexual attraction, how to become sexier in old age, how to realize one's sex potential. There are books and magazines galore, sold under the counter in most bookstores, which describe in grisly detail how to enjoy every aspect of sex, even the sexual violation of children between the ages of three and six. The exponents of so-called "liberated sex" are encouraging all this, as are the purveyors of pornography who are making millions of dollars out of this filthy trash. As a reaction to this pornography boom whole communities are starting anti-pornography campaigns.

Another reaction to it seems to be a boom in virginity novels. Barbara Cartland, a successful writer of romances, said in an interview in the New York Times:

The romantic age, which began two years ago, took writers, composers, publishers, theatrical, film producers by surprise. In the past two years, the sales of my novels have leaped into astronomical figures and have now reached 70 million. 26 new novels will appear in Britain this year. I am a best seller in Europe, North

America and also Turkey, Singapore, India, the Phillipines and Sri Lanka. Why? Because all my heroines are virgins.

The demand is not surprising in the East, where men have always insisted and expected their women to be pure, but this wild enthusiasm from the West is unprecedented.

I have yet to meet a man who did not want his wife to be different from the "good time" girls with whom he amuses himself. I have yet to talk to a woman who doesn't long for an overwhelming, ecstatic love from a man who worships her as his ideal and his inspiration.

The pendulum will swing as it always does, and in five to ten years time it will be fashionable to be a virgin. It is then we will go back to high standards, noble ideals and decency. They all begin on a foundation of female chastity. The reason we have pornography at all is entirely due to women failing to do their job as the guardians of morals.

The whole process is symbolized by the image employed in every religion, that of the virgin. It is not only an attribute of the body, it is a state of mind.

In their efforts to be free, modern and the equals of men, women have thrown away not only their virginity but also their mystique.*

It is strangely significant that throughout history there seem to have been three attitudes toward the body. First we read about the cult of the body which was developed by the Greeks; perfection of the physical body was something to be worshipped. True, in ancient pagan societies there were temple prostitutes and various kinds of mysterious religions which prostituted the body and urged its devotees to engage in various erotic practices. There was also widespread homosexuality. On the other hand, there were the vestal virgins of ancient Rome and the virginal Delphic Oracle. Virginity was required of those who were entrusted with prophecy and mystical insight.

*Barbara Cartland, *The New York Times,* April 15, 1977; © 1977 by The New York Times Company. Reprinted by permission.

There has also been an era (which was a protest against the over-exaltation of the physical body) of denial of the body. Some of the extreme ascetics of all religions have subjected the body to various kinds of physical torments such as hair shirts, self-flagellation, standing in ice cold water for hours in prayer, sitting on beds of nails.

There needs to be a balance here between an over-indulgence of the body and an over-denial of the body if we are to become prayerful people.

And so we come to the great people of our Christian faith. I am thinking particularly of Mary who we are told was a fifteen-year-old virgin in deep and devoted prayer when the angel Gabriel appeared to her and told her she was to be the mother of God. Then there is the example of Joseph, her fiancé, who was told by God that he must not live with her or even approach her sexually until after Jesus had been born. The Roman Catholic Church still believes that Joseph denied himself sexually throughout his life in order to protect Mary as the bride of God and the mother of God's son; consequently he has been sainted by that Church.

Then there is Jesus Himself. There is no reference anywhere to Jesus as anything but chaste. He was totally chaste in all his relationships with the men and women who are mentioned in the New Testament and to whom He ministered. His body was the temple of the Holy Spirit in every respect.

The greatest of the saints whose lives were committed to poverty, obedience and chastity were mostly creative celibates. They deliberately denied the desires of the body and the lusts of the flesh in order to keep themselves truly the temple of the Holy Spirit. They deliberately lived in great austerity, in great simplicity and in poverty. Their cells were often small, cold and uncomfortable. Their food was simple and organic. They fasted and prayed constantly and they built the great abbeys and cathedrals of the Age of Faith in

Europe. They illuminated the Bible with immortal art; they wrote, played and sang great music. They were great orators and witnesses to their faith in and love for their Lord and Savior to whom they had offered everything they had. In the case of most of them, in spite of their self-imposed austerity and simplicity and discipline of life, they were astonishingly healthy when one considers the lack of knowledge of modern scientific medicine and the prevalence of great plagues that periodically swept Europe in the Middle Ages. They wrote immortal verse, histories and prayers. One thinks of the great prayer poems of St. Columba of Iona, the history of the English Church by the Venerable Bede, and the hymns of the Irish saints.

I am wondering what would happen in today's age if the pendulum swung from our cult of food, drink and sex to a preoccupation with truly making the body once again a temple of the Holy Spirit in the excited hope that the Holy Spirit would cultivate our bodies, souls, minds and emotions in the creative and marvelous ways of God, just as He did with the great saints of history.

There are millions of decent, God-fearing single women in the world who do not wish to "sleep around," who somehow or other believe in chastity and romance and yet are frustrated because they cannot find any adequate creative outlet for their energies and imaginations or their soul capacities. There are many men suffering from the same frustrations.

There are millions of widows who, because they do not wish to marry again, too often become doormats to their children and grandchildren instead of making an exciting, adventurous contribution to society. I would like to suggest to all these people that they take their dusty souls, minds and imaginations off the shelf in the temple which is their bodies; dust them off, offer them to God, go to their knees in fasting and prayer and see what exciting things might happen in them and through them.

When St. Paul described the body as a temple of the Spirit,

he was talking of the most beautiful religious building known to man—the Jewish Temple in Jerusalem. This glorious temple, the Jews' lodestar, was built carefully according to designs given to Solomon and carried on in the minds and hearts of Jews throughout the centuries. If St. Paul likens our bodies to a temple, which is the holiest place of worship for the Jews, he was talking about something beautiful, holy, inspiring, filled with worship, filled with praise, filled with glory, filled with mystery, filled with God. He is telling us with this wonderful imagery that this is what our bodies can be.

We people who are single or widowed or, through choice, "celibate," need not feel like fifth wheels. God's plan for us is fulfillment. He who created us and loved us through all the vicissitudes of our lives still has wonderful adventures in store for us right into and through the doors of death. I am a widow, my husband has been dead for thirteen years; I have not wished to remarry. I have not wished to become my childrens' babysitter. Since my conversion to Christ fifty years ago my life's vocation has increasingly become intercessory prayer. I have spoken about it in all kinds of groups across the United States and the world. I truly believe that intercessory prayer is the great door-opener into people's hearts, homes, communities, churches and countries. I feel truly alive and creative.

There are millions of married people in the world who are disciplined in their sex lives because they realize that to be truly united in Christ and truly effective in their prayers and witness, they must honor not only their own but each other's bodies.

What is keeping you from making your body the temple of the Holy Spirit? Is it overindulgence in sex, liquor, hostile thoughts, self-pity, aimless pleasure seeking, ambition, scorn of other people, or self-righteousness? I have known self-pity and angry thoughts and ambition and lack of purpose and scorn and self-righteousness. Any one of these can clutter up the temple of our bodies. That is why the Christian Church has always put strong emphasis on repentance and confession. In the early Church this confession was often public. Now we go to psychiatrists who cannot offer us God's forgiveness and grace.

The loving God to whom we pray wants fellowship with us. Because we know He is good and righteous, our sin, our failure to make the body the temple of the spirit, prevents intimate communion. The block is ours, not His.

This morning, while I was participating in the Holy Communion, I had a flash of insight into one of its deepest meanings, one which relates very closely to the idea that the body is the temple of the Holy Spirit. When we come to Communion, we come in our bodies and as we go to the altar rail to receive His body and blood, we receive the bread of His own body into our bodies, the blood of His own body into our bodies and souls. In other words, we exchange our own bodies and minds and spirits for His. This is a great mystery, and this is why it is so difficult for so many of us to understand the full and awe-inspiring meaning of the Holy Communion. We have cleansed and prepared and opened the door of this house in which we dwell and invited Him to come in and occupy it. So here again we see the tremendous significance of St. Paul's great statement: "The body is the temple of the Holy Spirit." If we expect to be filled with the spirit, power and love of God, we must receive Him into our faulty bodies after confession, penitence and cleansing so that He can go in and out of this temple of ourselves and through us heal and encourage, comfort and strengthen others.

Whether we are young or old, married or single, rich or poor, we are to treat our bodies with reverence as fit places in which His wonderful, flaming Holy Spirit can live and move and have His being. Then we can expect to see the answer to our prayers, because He, our Lord, has promised it, and He, our Lord, wishes to dwell in us.

"Many are called and few are chosen."

"Ye have not chosen me, I have chosen
you, and ordained you, that ye should go
and bring forth fruit and that your fruit
should remain."

ST. JOHN 15:16

❋❉❉❉❉❉❉❉❉❉❉❉❉❉❉❉❉❉❉❉❉❉❉❉❉❉❋

8 ❋ THE MYSTERY OF BEING
CALLED AND CHOSEN

THE Almighty Creator, the Father, *chose* to create man
in His own image. The Bible is full of "chosens." I have already referred to Jacob wrestling with the angel and being
chosen to be "Israel." We have the story of Joseph who was
chosen to go down into Egypt and perform a great work there
for his God. We have the story of Esther, the wonderful Jewish queen of Persia, who was chosen at great risk to her own
life to save her people from annihilation. When she shrank
from her choosing, Mordecai, her foster father, said to her
sternly, "Who knowest but what thou hast been called to the
kingdom for such a time as this?" We have the story of
Daniel, who was chosen to reveal to several kings the mighty
will of God through the interpretation of dreams and visions.
We have the story of Ezra and Zerubbabel and the latter
prophets, who were chosen by God to further His purposes

for His people. Of course Jesus is the ultimate "chosen," being one with the Father Himself.

Before we can be chosen we must be called; however, many are called but few are chosen. Perhaps all of God's created beings are called in one way or another to do their part in weaving the great tapestry of His purpose. But many of them who are called refuse the call and consequently miss the opportunity and the responsibility of being chosen.

I have always been bothered by the daring challenge of Jesus, "Strait is the gate and narrow is the way that leadeth unto salvation, and few there be that go in thereat." Only those who trust in God's infinite grace and love and plan dare to go through that strait gate so that they may be chosen to do His purposes.

So there it is: we are each called to play a part in God's great drama of redemption.

What have you been called to do and have you responded so that you may be chosen?

Recently I discovered in my files two amazing letters from two women who responded to the call. The first letter is from a woman who could be any one of us. The second is from "the Late Liz," Gert Behanna, who wrote me in 1948 just after she had been called and chosen. She died several months ago and there are few individuals who have reached as many American men and women as "the Late Liz." Almost her last act on earth was to win to Christ a young black man who came seeking; as he sat on her bed as she lay dying she introduced him to her Lord and his.

LETTER ONE

I became a converted Christian just a year and a half ago, though I had been brought up in the Episcopal Church and attended church and Sunday school regularly. As I remember it there was much to-do about Christian virtues and good works, which to me are the fruits of Christianity, but the seed, the Christ Spirit, was never planted. So none of it sank very deep.

I didn't start giving religion serious thought until I went to college, and then it was because I was learning things that seemed to oppose what I had at least accepted in the past. From psychology I learned what motivates men's actions. The social sciences especially taught me that people's ideas of what is good and what is bad depend on the society or culture in which they live, and that everything is relative, nothing is absolute, etc. . . . Then I learned how man's conception of God has changed through the ages, and I decided that God was just something that man had made up to explain his existence; an explanation that was no longer necessary. At this time I had a strange and sudden accident which made me feel that life had no meaning or value.

You can imagine the effect that such attitudes would have on a person. I didn't like to be alone, and I kept up a restless kind of activity so that I wouldn't have to think too much. And every once in awhile the most disturbing feelings would come over me, of complete emptiness and futility, and a great loneliness. I felt that all men were basically cut off and separate from each other; there could never by any real or permanent bond between them.

After college I went to a strange city to live. I was very lonely and I couldn't get the kind of job I expected to get. I started thinking of people I had known in the past who seemed to have a kind of power over life—Christian Scientists and followers of New Thought teachings. Their faith struck me as being no more than a mental discipline, and I didn't see why I couldn't develop that kind of faith to get what I wanted. So I bought myself a book on the power of constructive thinking, and went to work. Sure enough, before long I was offered a wonderful job where I made a number of dear friends. I was very happy.

But I had built my house upon sand, and in time it crumbled, leaving me completely bewildered, confused and frightened. I was afraid of everything and everyone, but most of all of my own fear, because I couldn't understand it. I knew that if there really was a God, he would have to give me true faith and true strength. So I prayed. And God answered my prayer. There came a series of persons and places and books which I seemed compelled to read which revealed to me what I needed to know at just the time I needed it.

My whole life has changed. It now has meaning, and purpose and direction. It's as if finding God were finding the key piece to a giant jigsaw puzzle, so that all the pieces fit in together to make a perfect whole. Every aspect of my life is so much more abundant, intangible, in material ways as well as spiritual.

But what astonishes me the most is the way in which I have changed, so gradually that I didn't even know it was happening. I no longer feel that I am a separate entity, but that we are all one; members of One Body and of each other. This results in a great sense of responsibility for all that is sad and evil in the world, and a great concern. And I feel that if I try to be a better and happier person I am somehow raising the whole level of humanity, and making it easier for other people to be better and happier. Then I feel a love in me that is greater than anything I have ever felt before, or that I think I am capable of feeling by myself.

I think that the fate of the world depends upon people finding what I have found. There are so many in the same position I was in such a short time ago, who have never even been exposed to a faith that works. I am not nearly as concerned about the atom bomb as I am about the slower, quieter ways in which people destroy themselves—essentially because they have lost contact with the source of life.

Diane

LETTER TWO

Calvary House
New York
April, 1948

Dear Helen,

Without gestures—for me—this will be quite a job. The shock of the simplicity of God's desires as compared to my own involved will is too overwhelming for facile words. I certainly do not intend to imply that I am doing His will—just that I see it and shall *some* day do it! Here goes!

I now know, by cut-but-never-read articles, by listed-but-never-purchased books, most of all by a mounting self-distaste—that the

Spirit of God has been working in me for several years. But I would not let Him through. Of course I didn't recognize Him—I felt the status quo was intolerable. Not *me*—oh, no, not me! I believed in God but in somewhat the same manner that a young person would anticipate—in the distant future—an old age pension. Some day I'd get around to God! Whew! So, riddled with fears, sick in soul and body, I just by chance met Tom and Blanche Page [a businessman and his wife, members of Calvary Episcopal Church in New York] in July of '47. I had heard something of the great changes which conversion had brought to them so almost immediately I literally attacked them—strangers—with my own problems. (If I had a collar on, it would now begin to tighten.) What a picture of intolerance, self-pity, criticism and arrogance I handed them! They didn't have to wonder—I *told* them that all my immediate world was wrong because it refused to be governed by me. What an exposé! The Pages listened and finally Tom was able to get in one little question. It was: "Gert, why don't you just turn the whole thing over to God?" It was slipped gently in and with a friendly humor—and it *staggered* me, literally. It was my very first introduction to the simplicity of God. I gaped at him and said, "Why, you say that just as you might tell me that my suitcase was too heavy—and I ought to get a Red Cap!" "That's exactly what I mean," Tom answered.

The rest of the evening is a little blurry but I do know that *I* was definitely not in the driver's seat. Ten days later I drove back to Illinois—that little question constantly burrowing into my consciousness: "Why don't you turn it over to God?" No more lip service; no more rationalizing; no more alibis; no more fears! It was very tempting! But *how?* I knew I was sick with *my* path but where was God's? The rusted door was beginning to creak open. And that old, old story—for the first time in my life—everywhere I went, others too seemed to be wondering about God. Heretofore not at all in social good taste!

I reached home late in July and found the Pages had mailed me the July-August "Evangel" and "Faith that Works." That did it, Helen. Between Sam and Horace Lukens, the old self-important Gert capitulated. No one, certainly not I, can put a rainbow or an evening star, or the forgiveness of God into words! The dam burst.

Within twenty mortal minutes, my tightened clutch had been loosened and God moved in! He didn't find His new tenant neat and shiny but He did find her willing. Some of the old furniture has had to be thrown out completely, parts have been re-done and will work. Certainly *everyone* is helping me with unbelievable generosity of spirit to find and test new "pieces" for my new abode.

The old Gent with the gay, red suit and the cold eyes still hovers around but now I recognize him. He's increasingly disgruntled too, I find. God's demand seems to me a pretty simple one. He only wants us to love Him and *to prove it*. Certainly old habits are hard to break. I know that every day but I also know my goal.

May God bless you and Sam and Calvary, Helen. And may He help us to help you.

> Gratefully,
> That uninhibited Gert
> (Behanna)

What a chain reaction, Sam and I obeyed God's call to us so we were chosen to introduce Diane to God, Tom and Blanche Page obeyed God's call and were chosen to call Gert Behanna, and she was chosen to reach thousands upon thousands for her Lord.

Recently I met a beautiful young woman at a prayer conference where Charles Colson shared with us his prison prayer experiences. She was involved in prison work herself and was so vividly alive that I asked her to write me an account of how she had been called and chosen for this work.

As a teenager it was very difficult for me to believe that God loved me, when I looked at my life and compared it to the lives of my friends. I felt very strongly that if my life was any example of God's love, I better stay away from him, because I might get into real trouble if he should take a dislike.

My mother and father were married in New York City; he was a stock broker and they were high fliers. They saw every Al Jolsen opening at the Wintergarden, went to the Dempsey-Tunney fights, had plenty of money, and everything was marvelous. That is until 1929. My father tried to buy when the Crash began and was wiped out. They came home to my mother's mother in Baltimore. Two years later I was born. My father had returned to his first profession, civil engineering; and they were beginning to get back on their feet. One year after my birth my father had a severe pain in his stomach. The doctor diagnosed indigestion; unfortunately the doctor was wrong, and my father died from a ruptured appendix in 1932. My mother, after collapsing at the graveside, began slyly and secretly, to drink.

Of course in the thirties, no family much less a southern one would admit that a woman in the family was drinking so everybody ignored it as it got worse and worse. Mother managed to save out enough money to buy a row house and convert the upper floors into apartments. This was so she could get out from under the watchful eye of my grandmother.

By the time I was nine years old, mother was beginning her day at 6:30 A.M. with a double shot of bourbon and a bottle of beer. She wasn't a happy drunk or a sleepy drunk. She was a belligerent drunk, because she was so desperately unhappy. In her frustration she would most often strike out at me, until I became old enough to hit back. It was at this time that I faced the fact that I could no longer invite anyone home with me, because in my home there was a succession of uncles—men that mother told me to call Uncle Tom, or Uncle Dick, or Uncle Harry. I remember very well my ninth birthday, when she gave me a watch in the morning and stole it back in the afternoon to pawn. When I was ten, she sold my dog. Periodically I would come home to find all my clothes dumped in the hall, because she had needed money and had rented my room out temporarily. Then she would suggest that I go visit my grandmother for a while until she got a little bit ahead. Of course all during my childhood and teenaged years, I would go places and hear people whisper, "That's her daughter."

When I was eleven—with a current Uncle Dick—she took me to New York for a week. We stayed at the St. George Hotel in a suite. I had a marvelous time. Uncle Dick would give me $20.00 or $25.00 a day to go out on the town as long as I stayed out all day. I could come home to the suite at dinner time and have a tray sent up to the room. I was generally awakened in the early hours of the morning when they would come home quarreling. I was eleven years old, it was wartime New York—1942, and I did New York all by myself. Of course at the time I thought I was alone, but now I know the Holy Spirit was keeping very special watch on a little girl by herself, because I never had an unpleasant experience.

I remember at fourteen, after an episode with my mother, when she would scream and throw glasses, dishes, or anything that came to hand, getting down on my knees to pray. I prayed with all my heart that God would kill my mother.

And so my teenage years passed. Those wonderful years that people warn you will never return—thank God. Mother was drunk at my sixth-grade graduation, drunk at my ninth-grade graduation, and drunk when I graduated from high school. It is hard for me now to remember the white hot intensity with which I hated her and how much I wished her dead. I could not see any possible reason to believe there was a God, much less that God loved me.

A new preacher came to the church across the street. He didn't have much trouble realizing that the girl across the street was in great need. He and his wife came after me. When they first came to visit, I couldn't have been more bored by what I thought were their ridiculous statements but like most people I did accord to those who come in the name of the Lord a certain surface respect. The thing different about these people, Southern Baptists, was that they kept coming. They didn't give up.

I am sure they were led by the Holy Spirit to challenge my mind. I was very proud of being "smart." Dr. Pearce dared me to make a test. For two years he asked me to pray every day—"God, I don't believe you're there; if you are there, please show yourself to me. Amen." For two years, I was to read a chapter of the Bible every day, starting with the New Testament. And for two years, I was to go to the church of Jesus Christ every Sunday. Somehow he also managed to get me to read *The Screwtape Letters* by C. S. Lewis. He told me that there was no way I could do this test without missing here and there because of Satan. I scoffed at such foolishness and began the test to prove the preacher wrong. After all at the end of two years, I would still have plenty of time left to do it my way. It was such an easy thing to do. The prayer wouldn't take thirty seconds; I was a fast reader so surely I could whip through a chapter of the Bible in four minutes; and an hour on Sunday would just have to be endured. Of course I didn't realize that the minister and his wife were praying daily for me.

And so I began the test. It was strange. I began the test to prove the preacher wrong, then as so many things happened to try to stop me; I continued the test to spite the devil.

One night at the end of twenty-two months, I prayed, got into bed and the Holy Spirit came for me. A presence, a power, a force—I know it was there. It filled the room. It was not warm or particularly loving. It was raw, naked power; and it filled every corner of the room. As I was pressed back into the bed, I said, "I believe." I have never looked back; I know what happened to me that night. God called me that night and changed my life. He took a young woman and changed everything about her; he changed the way I talk, he changed the way I look, he changed the way I think and above all he changed the things I love. God called me that night and changed—me.

I began my adventure with the Lord with such enthusiasm. After my experience with the Holy Spirit, I jumped into the life of the Church with both feet. I was first asked to help in the junior department of the Vacation Bible School. What a wonderful place for a person who knows little about the Church or Bible to begin—the literal, fundamental juniors. Next, I began to teach juniors in Sunday School and Training Union. Don't think I didn't point out to God all I was doing for Him. Of course, the one learning the most was—me. My period of training continued for seventeen years. The marvelous thing was that I always considered the thing at hand the most important thing I could possibly be doing.

Then one night, while praying, I heard—clear as a bell—"Ann, why don't you go to those who need to hear what happened to you." I immediately thought of those in prison. So often people in prison do not have a father and are surrounded by alcoholism, homosexuality, etc. I contacted my minister. We had a prison ministry of sorts, and they were delighted to have me join them. I would speak once a month to about sixty women in the city jail. I was always well received, because I wasn't a fake. The subconscious always makes contact, and they knew that when I told them about my youth and how I came to Christ that I was for real. And so for three years I would stand up and speak about my experiences with the Lord.

It was at this time that the riots occurred in Attica. All volunteer work at the prisons was stopped. I prayed over what I should do now. I didn't feel any impetus whatsoever to go back to teaching in the Church—and so I waited. I tried several times to get back into prison work. One morning I received a call from the social services department of my county. They were asking for volunteers. I told them that I was very interested in doing volunteer work in the prisons. When they asked what I did, and I told them that I witnessed for Christ; they felt it would be better if I waited for them to call me. Time passed. One morning I received a call from Mr. C. of The State Training School for Boys. They were allowing volunteers to return to the prisons; and when he had called my county to see if they had any extra volunteers they didn't need, he was given my name. He asked what I did. When I told him that I witnessed for Christ, there was a long silence. He explained that the training school housed boys from the inner city—mainly black boys. He doubted that they would sit still for a white woman talking about Jesus. I suggested that he give me a chance. It was arranged that I would go up to the school—a distance of about forty miles—one Monday. I arrived to find four men waiting to observe exactly what it was that I did. They took me to a cottage, and I spoke to a group of thirty boys. The boys sat in rapt silence and gave me complete attention. I was taken into about six more cottages with only time out for lunch. At 4:30 P.M. Mr. C. asked if I would come up every week and talk to the boys in the two maximum security cottages. He explained that I would not have any insurance at the school, because I was a volunteer. I assured him that my insurance rested with a higher authority. So I began four and one half years ago to tell young men fifteen to eighteen years old about how much God loved them and about what He had done for me.

Over a year ago I went to a party and talked with the head of the F.B.I. in my area. He remarked that I certainly must have heard some ripe language in my work. I assured him that, even though I talked with the boys in gymnasiums quite removed from the guards and frequently had groups of twenty-five or more, I had not heard so much as a "hell." He was stunned. Later he called me and asked if I would go and talk to a Ms. B. She was the highest ranking woman in the state penal system. An appointment was made, and Ms. B. allocated me one half hour. I talked with her for almost two hours, and she took me on a tour of the state penitentiary. She asked if I would be willing to come every Monday and talk with men who were first offenders. I would tell them what had happened to me—using not only my personal experience, but the sustaining power of the Holy Spirit to give them some hope. And so I became the first woman in the field of religion to work with men in the state penal system. It was thrilling to be granted the privilege of witnessing every week of my life to the power, glory and above all love of my Savior, Jesus Christ, to people who need him so much.

God chose me to do something only because I love Him. I didn't begin serving my Lord in prison; I began with the juniors in a Vacation Bible School. Doors opened for me to serve God; I chose to go through some of them. In this process, I learned and became capable of doing something else. I would guess that if I had not chosen to go through those first doors I would never have had the chance to do the work I am doing now. I wouldn't have had the knowledge and Bible background to handle the questions that are fired at me constantly. It is the first little decision that you make that sends you along a path: and as you make each decision, He sends you down another path and your life work emerges.

Is God calling you? Are you saying "Yes" to Him so that He may choose you to call others, that they in turn may call still others? It's like mining diamonds; you may be chosen to mine lots of small diamonds and then suddenly you will mine a great diamond. Many are called and *some* are chosen. Will you be among the chosen?

"Whatsoever ye shall ask the Father in my
name, He will give it to you. Hitherto ye
have asked nothing in my name: ask, and ye
shall receive, that your joy may be full."

ST. JOHN 16:23–24

᙭⚜⚜⚜⚜⚜⚜⚜⚜⚜⚜⚜⚜⚜⚜⚜⚜⚜⚜⚜᙭

9 ⚜ THE MYSYERY OF
PRAYER IN JESUS' NAME

ANOTHER of the mysterious things that happens to us is
connected with prayer in His name or *of* His name, which we
are told over and over again we must use. To pray in His
name has been variously interpreted, but only recently have a
number of us experimented with it.

In ancient times the name of a god, a king or a kingdom
represented the essence of that god or king or kingdom. Zeus
for instance, meant the god of thunder; Aphrodite, the
goddess of love; Apollo, the god of the sun and of light;
Diana, the goddess of the hunt. The name of a people was
exceedingly important and still is, as is the name of a nation.
Immense importance was placed on the name "Israel." God
named Jacob "Israel." The name "Israel" represented this
people as it still does.

The name "American" represents those of us who are
Americans.

The name "Swiss" represents those of us who are Swiss.

The name of a person or a group is enormously important,

such as the name "Christian" which describes the disciples of Jesus. Bishop Pardue, the retired Episcopal Bishop of Pittsburg says, "We have the Supreme Name in the Name of Jesus. Are we using it as we should?"

The Orthodox have developed as a special prayer of power "Lord Jesus Christ, Son of the Living God, have mercy on me a sinner," or just the word, *Jesus*. Orthodox Christians say this prayer hourly and daily over and over until it becomes a very part of their breathing; and as to breathe is to live, this prayer, as we breathe in and out, permeates our inner selves and the air around us with the life of Jesus.

A friend of mine has been experimenting with me in praying this "Jesus Prayer." One night she was saying the Jesus Prayer over and over again, applying it not only to herself but to the people who were in her heart, and suddenly she saw a blinding light at the foot of her bed and a voice seemed to be saying to her, "Look at this Light!" Something inside of her told her that, if she looked at this Light and continued the prayer in obedience to the voice in her soul, she would die. And the voice said to her gently, "Yes, you will die to yourself but you will live to me." She looked at the Light and she had the same strange experience of ecstasy that I had when I made my surrender to God, and it came about as she said the Jesus Prayer because to truly pray in His name is to pray in His person, in His very nature and, in a mysterious way, when we do this we are caught up into Him. Our prayer is fused with His eternal prayer for us and we experience the prayer He prayed for us in that Upper Room so long ago: "I in Them and Thou in me, that they also may be one in us: that the world may believe that thou hast sent me" (St. John 17:20).

In an illuminating book called *The Way of a Pilgrim,* which is the story of a simple Russian peasant's experience with the Jesus Prayer, we read of how the pilgrim visits great Orthodox monasteries all over Russia and sits at the feet of holy monks whose lives are permeated with the Jesus Prayer. They throw flashing light on both the outward and inward power of prayer.

The abbot or skhimnik of one of these monasteries has a dialogue with the pilgrim. He says to him, "Prayer brings a man to a new birth, as it were. Its power is so great that nothing, no degree of suffering will stand against it. Prayer is so powerful, so mighty, that pray, and do what you like." Prayer will guide you to right and just action. In order to please God, nothing more is needed than love. "Love, and do what you will," says the blessed Augustine, "for he who truly loves cannot wish to do anything which is not pleasing to the one he loves." Since prayer is the outpouring and the activity of love, then one can truly say of it similarly, "Nothing more is needed for salvation than continuous prayer."

1. "Pray, and *think* what you will," your thoughts will be purified by prayer. Prayer will give you enlightenment of mind; it will remove and drive away all ill-judged thoughts. "Overcome the foes in your mind by the Name of Jesus. You will find no other weapon than this."

2. "Pray, and *do* what you will." Your acts will be pleasing to God and useful and salutary to yourself. Frequent prayer, whatever it may be about, does not remain fruitless, because in it is the power of grace, "for whosoever shall call on the Name of the Lord shall be saved" (Acts 11:21).

3. "Pray, and do not labour much to conquer your passions by your own strength." Prayer will destroy them in you. "For greater is He that is in you than he that is in the world" (I John 1:4). And St. John Karpathisky teaches that if you have not the gift of self-control, do not be cast down, but know that God requires of you diligence in prayer and the prayer will save you.

4. "Pray, and fear nothing." Fear no misfortunes, fear no disasters. Prayer will protect you and ward them off. Remember St. Peter, who had little faith and was sinking; St. Paul, who prayed in prison. . . .

5. Pray somehow or other, only pray always and be disturbed by nothing. Be gay in spirit and peaceful. Prayer will arrange every-

thing and teach you. Remember what the saints—John Chrysostom and Mark the Podvizhnik—say about the power of prayer. The first declares that prayer, even though it be offered by us who are full of sin, cleanses us at once. The latter says: "To pray somehow is within our power but to pray purely is the gift of grace." So offer to God what it is within your power to offer. Bring to Him at first just quantity (which is within your power) and God will pour upon you strength in your weakness. "Prayer, dry and distracted may be, but continuous, will establish a habit and become second nature and turn itself into prayer which is pure, luminous, flaming and worthy."

6. It is to be noted, finally, that if the time of your vigilence in prayer is prolonged, then naturally no time will be left not only for doing sinful actions but even for thinking of them.

Now do you see what profound thoughts are focused in that wise saying: "Love, and do what you will"; "Pray, and do what you will"? How comforting and consoling is all this for the sinner overwhelmed by his weaknesses, groaning under the burden of his warring passions.

Prayer—there you have the whole of what is given to us as the universal means of salvation and of the growth of the soul into perfection. Just that. But when prayer is named, a condition is added. "Pray without ceasing" is the command of God's word. Consequently prayer shows its most effective power and fruit when it is offered often, ceaselessly; for frequency of prayer undoubtedly belongs to our will, just as purity, zeal and perfection in prayer are the gift of grace.

And so we will pray as often as we can; we will consecrate our whole life to prayer, even if it be subject to distractions to begin with. Frequent practice of it will teach us attentiveness. Quantity will certainly lead on to quality.*

And as Jesus tells the disciples, "What soever ye ask the Father in my name, He will give it to you. Hitherto ye have asked nothing in My Name: ask, and ye shall receive, that your joy may be full" (St. John 16:23–24).

* R. M. French, trans., *The Way of a Pilgrim* (New York: The Seabury Press, 1965), pp. 207–209.

10 ✤ THE MYSTERY OF
PRAYER AND COINCIDENCES

I HAVE said in an earlier book that prayer is love in action. If we *care* for people, or about our communities or our nation or our world, we will, as the old hymn goes, "take them to the Lord in Prayer." Next to our love for God we will love our neighbor and how better to show our love for our neighbor than to pray for him or her. Then starts the miracle of God's intervention and God-inspired coincidences. William Temple, the great Archbishop of Canterbury, had a famous saying: "When I pray, coincidences happen."

I have seen this statement acted out so often that I know it is true. All of us know of the great organization which aids alcoholics called Alcoholics Anonymous. Most of us do not know how it originated; initially, God chose three men who did not know each other to be instruments in its founding. One person was the very well known superintendent of a rescue mission in the Bowery in New York City named Hadley. This man had been, as he described it, "rescued from sin and drink." During his entire ministry there, he prayed daily for a son who had inherited his alcoholism and who had disappeared. The son never came back during Mr. Hadley's lifetime, but Mr. Hadley did not stop praying. When he died, the son happened to read in a newspaper in another city that his father had died. He came back, and as he knelt beside his father's casket, he was marvelously transformed from a hopeless drunk to a redeemed man. He was led almost immediately to look for some way in which to found a mission like his father's. Quite understandably, the Bowery mission was leery of trusting the superintendency to this untried young man. Meanwhile, a young rector, Sam Shoemaker, who had just assumed the pastorship of an Episcopal parish in downtown New York, was walking past the closed chapel of the church in what is known as the gashouse district on East 23rd Street and asking God what he wanted him to do about that closed chapel. For some years the church had been running a flophouse for drunks—euphemistically called "The Olive Tree Inn"—where a drunk would come in and get a cup of coffee and mattress to sleep on, but that is all that particular church knew about helping drunks. The chapel remained closed until the young rector began to pray and ask God what to do. God told him very clearly, "You are to open a rescue mission in that chapel. I will send you someone to run it because I know you don't know anything about alcoholism, not having been an alcoholic yourself. However, this is my will. You will get the money, and I will send you the superintendent." That very day the young redeemed drunk, Harry Hadley, was led to walk into Sam Shoemaker's office, having heard of Calvary Church and its closed chapel. Sam sized him up, told him he would try and get the money to open the chapel and start a rescue mission. In a few week's time, Sam's vestry had granted him the money to do this. Mr. Hadley was hired and installed, and during the ten years that this rescue mission operated down there in the gashouse district on East 23rd Street where the drunks were all over the sidewalks, 250,000 of them came through the doors of that chapel and 40,000 of them were truly redeemed. Harry Hadley and Sam Shoemaker met in daily prayer for this undertaking as did some members of the vestry; one night a drunk named Bill, who had been doing the saloons up and down Third Avenue, staggered in, sat through the little service, was clear enough in the head to hear the altar call and went forward. He didn't stay sober long because he was so elated over his experience that he felt he had to celebrate. Fortunately, before he got too drunk he went to a Dr. Silkworth's sanitarium whose business it was to dry out drunks. When Dr. Silkworth got through with him, he sent him down to Sam Shoemaker, whose business it was to train laymen for Christian witness. Bill lived at our church house during that time. He slipped once or twice. On one occasion Sam dressed him down so hard and Bill got so angry that he threw an alarm clock through his bedroom window; it landed on the stained-glass window of the church above the altar, so that when Sam went to celebrate communion next morning he saw a large alarm clock staring at him. He went upstairs and hauled Bill out of bed and showed him what he had done, and Bill was so overwhelmed at this blasphemy that this time he decided it was no more liquor for keeps.

One morning he was sitting in Sam's study, and he said, "Sam, drunks need some guidelines to live by like your lay persons do." "You write me some," said Sam looking at him shrewdly. "Bill, I am not a drunk. You know what drunks need because you have been one. Go and sit down in the sitting room out there and ask the Lord to give you a set of guidelines for drunks." Bill looked at Sam with surprise and considerable consternation, but he did as he was bid, and in twenty minutes the Holy Spirit had dictated to Bill the twelve steps of Alcoholics Anonymous which has been the AA's Bible to this day.

Sam was obedient to the guidance of the Holy Spirit and founded a rescue mission in the gashouse district of New York, into which Bill W., the founder of AA, was nudged by

God so many years ago. And because Bill was obedient to the guidance of the Holy Spirit when he sat down to write the twelve steps, the movement of Alcoholics Anonymous was born. Due to this mighty movement, which has spread across the globe, millions of men and women who have been hopeless alcoholics have been cured and set on the road to a full life. All because three men prayed and listened and God in His mercy led a drunk into a rescue mission where he received the "grace" to give it up. Mysterious, wonderful, coincidental. Planned by God to reach these unhappy children of His at this particular time in history.

Recently I had a striking example of such a coincidence and the chain reaction that spins off from it. I spend my winters in Florida. A friend of mine and I were curious about a big paperback book store which had just opened in our Florida resort, so we visited it. We went to the counter and asked when Charles Colson's *Born Again* was to be sold there. I noticed two nicely dressed young men standing beside the counter and when I used the phrase "born again" one of the young men said, "Lady, are you born again?" I said, "Yes!" Then he said, "Well, we are too [pointing to his friend]. He is pastor of the First Baptist Church here, and I'm an evangelist and am preaching a revival mission for him. Have you ever heard of a preacher named Sam Shoemaker? Because I'm preaching on one of his theme songs, 'Get Changed, Get Together, Get Going.' " My friend who was standing beside me said quietly, "You happen to be speaking to Sam Shoemaker's widow." The young men's mouths fell open in speechless surprise as did the young man's at the checkout counter. So we went and had a cup of coffee together and they returned with us to my apartment where we had a time of in-depth prayer. The young pastor was discouraged and lonely and we prayed that some would respond to his eager challenge and bring him comfort and fellowship.

The story doesn't end there. Two nights later they visited a young couple who had not been attending the pastor's church and whose marriage was not thriving. The young evangelist talked right to their need and they asked the Lord to come into their hearts right there in their living room. The next night they both took the altar call and were "born again." The following week the wife went to the office of a cousin of mine who works for the local newspaper to place an ad in the paper. As they were talking about jobs, the wife said, "All I can do is type." My cousin knew I was looking for a typist to type this manuscript and she mentioned me to Jenny. That evening Jenny phoned me and I engaged her. The next morning Jenny arrived all ready for work. I asked her where she went to church and to my astonishment she said the First Baptist and I said, "Oh yes, that is where Mr. J. S. is holding revival services, isn't it?" Her eyes popped wide open and she said, "How did you know?" Then I told her my story of meeting her pastor and J. S., and how much I had enjoyed them. This gave her the courage to say shyly, "Two nights ago my husband and I were visited by the pastor and J. S. and we were born again." Then and there Jenny and I sat down, took hands and thanked God for our mutual faith in our Lord and for sending her to me so that I might give her fellowship and she might meet my need for typing help.

It wasn't long before Jenny's new found faith was severely tested. Some friends came for a visit and, instead of remaining a day, one of them got ill and they remained a week. For a young housewife with two young children this was an interruption in her household routine which was almost too much for her. The following week she arrived so tense and exhausted that she felt she had to give up her job. I said, "No Jenny, I doubt if this is right, let's have a prayer about this." I prayed, "Dear Lord, you know Jenny is a new Christian, and all this commotion in her house is exhausting her and making her tense and nervous. Please come to us now and give her the peace you promised, the peace that passes all understanding, so that this week will be a week of joy and quiet confidence in your power.''

Jenny decided to keep the job with me and the following week she returned, eyes shining, and said, ''Oh Mrs. Shoemaker, something so wonderful happened to me after our prayer. I feel all smoothed out. I was able to care for my friends and husband and children without strain, and my husband told me how proud he was of me.''

You see, the young evangelist and the young pastor had a need and God brought them across our path. My friend and I had a need to minister, and God used us to minister. Jenny had a need and God brought her to me, as I needed two young willing hands to help me. In the process He mysteriously bound six total strangers together in the mutually helpful support that only He can supply. How deeply true is the promise of St. Paul: ''My God shall supply all your need according to His riches in glory in Christ.'' And how mysteriously and coincidentally He has woven together six lives in *Him*.

This chain of coincidences has happened to me so often in my life that I know with Bishop Temple that when you pray coincidences happen.

After Sam Shoemaker prayed about that closed chapel, the coincidences began after direct intercession, then obedience. In the case of my experience in Florida, the chain reaction of coincidences began as the result of being obedient to the guidance of God's Holy Spirit and then intercession. Intercession, obedience and coincidence are illustrations of ''lived out prayer'' which is what gives the tingle of adventure to every Christian life.

"Man ought always to pray, and not to
faint."

LUKE 18:1

"And shall not God avenge his own elect,
which cry day and night unto him, though
he bear long with them."

LUKE 18:7

11 ❈ THE MYSTERY OF INTERCESSION AND INTERVENTION

"THE prayer of a righteous man availeth much."

We are told in the Bible of the prayers of a number of
righteous men and how in answer to their prayers God sent
His angels to intervene in their behalf.

When the prophet Elisha was at Dothan, the king of Syria
sent his army to take him prisoner. Elisha's servant saw the
army camped around the city. He rushed back to tell Elisha.
"And Elisha prayed, and said, 'Lord, I pray Thee, open his
eyes, that he may see.' And the Lord opened the young
man's eyes and 'behold the mountain was full of horses and
chariots of fire around Elisha' " (Kings 6:17). The angels in
God's armies were sent to intervene and save Elisha, God's
righteous man.

The Book of Daniel tells us the story of angelic intervention in the story of Shadrach, Meshach and Abednego, who were cast bound into the fiery furnace by King Nebuchadnezzar because they had dared to worship God against his decree. The king went to see that his orders were carried out, and to his astonishment he saw four men walking unharmed in the burning furnace and "the form of the fourth was like unto the Son of God." Then Nebuchadnezzar ordered that Shadrach, Meshach and Abednego be released from the furnace and said, "Blessed be the God of Shadrach, Meshach and Abednego, who hath sent his angel and delivered His servants that trusted in Him" (Daniel 3:19–30).

Again in the Book of Daniel, we have the story of Daniel, the Persian king's counselor, who was accused by jealous noblemen of praying to his God three times a day in defiance of the king. The king had made a law that anyone worshipping another god than the god he had decreed would be cast into a den of lions. So Daniel, his beloved high counselor, was thrown into a den of lions, because the king could not change his own law. The king didn't sleep that night; he came to the den of lions early in the morning to see if Daniel was still alive and cried out to him in distress, "O servant of the living God, is thy God whom thou servest continually, able to deliver thee from the lions?" And Daniel replied, "My God hath sent His angel, and hath shut the lions' mouths, and they have not hurt me" (Daniel 6:4–23).

There are many other such instances of God's mysterious intervention in response to the prayers of His people, in both the Old and New Testaments. But does He intervene today? Of course He does. If "God is the same yesterday, today, and forever," it isn't possible that His love for us has grown cold and that He will no longer send His angels to help us or intervene to change the circumstances around us in response to our prayer for help.

A friend of mine, a dedicated priest, received an emer-

gency call to come to his mother who lay desperately ill
in a county hospital. She and the family felt if he could only
get there and lay his hands on her for healing that she would
get well. So he quickly hopped into his rather ancient and
battered car and started out on a 250-mile trip in the dead of
summer. Suddenly he saw the heat gauge on his car rising
dangerously. He stopped at a gas station where the attendant
told him that he needed a new heat gauge and that the station
did not have any. So he knew he had to get to his mother
without help. Consequently, he began to pray fervently that
God would send an angel to help him so that he might arrive
on time. Then the mysterious miracle happened. The heat
gauge started to rise the moment he increased his speed and
suddenly it was checked. This took place for the rest of the
200 miles. He arrived in time to pray for and with his
mother, to lay his hands on her, and she was healed. Could
this illustrate that when God knows there is an acute need and
an answer to desperate and fervent prayer, He will send an
angel to help? The whole scripture promises this. How about
the great promise in Psalm 91, "For he shall give his angels
charge over thee, . . . they shall bear thee up in their hands,
lest thou dash thy foot against a stone." And how about Jesus'
great promise of help when we need it. He alone knows when
we do need it and when our urgent request is valid.

Most people know of the Iona Community in Scotland,
founded in 540 A.D. by the great Gaelic St. Columba who
refused a kingship, became a humble monk and evangelized
the whole of Scotland. Recently a dedicated group of Scottish
Presbyterians undertook to rebuild his ancient ruined monastery and establish a modern religious community dedicated to
the vision of St. Columba. They had built up the walls of the
monastery when World War II broke out, and there was no
timber allowed in the whole of the British Isles for the re-
building of the roof, so these valiant moderns went down on

their knees in prayer and shortly a Norwegian ship broke down and was blown out to the island.

When they went to salvage her they found that she was loaded with roof timbers exactly the right width and length for the completion of the roof. Was St. Columba himself watching over his people from high heaven and did he intervene or did God send an angel? Who knows, but what a wonderful and mysterious happening.

There are other happenings that can only be termed divine intervention.

A young friend of mine, a converted ex-convict, has started Christian fellowship work in the Los Angeles area to bring Christ's compassion to needy people one by one. They call themselves partners in Christ and he writes that one of the partners was named "Rick"—but I'll let him tell the story:

One of our new partners in Christ was Rick. He was beset with masses of serious troubles. Rick has been running a good-sized business selling drapes and carpets, and cleaning them with his father, sister and her husband. He sold part of his business to a man, who then failed to pay a cent of what he'd promised. The business was sunk in complex financial troubles, and had arrears of $15,000 to pay. Rick was sued by several companies.

Rick and I asked the Lord what to do, and He told us, "Put the whole business into My hands. Open your hearts and I'll show you My way out of your mess." So we turned our minds on Him and marched forward boldly with Him, following all His directions.

Rick got back the part of the business from the man who had defaulted. Bob, another loyal partner in Christ, worked full time to put the whole business on its feet. I gave whatever time I could spare from my other duties.

One day someone demanded that Rick make an urgent payment of $395 the very next day. We had no way to pay this. Rick's Dad threw up his hands in defeat. But Rick and I raised our hands to God, trusting He'd step in and help us. The mail next morning brought in a check for $400.00 which was *an advance payment for work we hadn't yet done.* That's God for you!

I have recently had two experiences of God's intervention in answer to prayer. For several months last autumn I suffered from what is known as Tacca cardia, an uneven heart beat. I had spent a weekend in the hospital, and been given new medication, some of which I had to stop because it disagreed with me. A number of friends were praying for me and then a wonderful thing happened. The Bishop of Coventry and his wife came to the Diocese of Maryland at the invitation of the Committee on Evangelism of which I was a member. I was their hostess because I was an old friend of the bishop. On the Sunday morning before the start of the mission, I asked the bishop if he would like to celebrate Holy Communion in my living room—just for him and his wife and a friend of mine. He knew of my need and shyly asked if I would like him to lay hands on me for healing. He had laid hands on me once before and I was healed. I knew he was a channel of healing power, so I gladly and gratefully assented. That living room of mine has been blessed forever by this and other occasions like it. As we shared the sacrament and as the Bishop laid his hands on me, we all felt a power flowing into us and reinvigorating us. I was able to go through the next few strenuous days without a quiver or one irregular heartbeat, through the Christmas season, and into the New Year. In fact, I've felt better than I have in a long time, in spite of a number of stressful problems which are part of the business of living.

The other intervention happened in Florida. At Christmas I received a Christmas card from a long lost cousin. I hadn't heard from her for ten years. Somehow she had found my address and wrote me that she was living in Ft. Myers Beach and hoped I was coming down again. I was overjoyed, as my father had been particularly fond of this young woman, and I knew she was "steel true and blade straight." So when I got to Ft. Myers I immediately looked her up. I found that she was sculpturing pelicans in bronze and ceramic for the commercial market. So I visited her in her studio and perched on a stool drinking tea at her kitchen counter. We eagerly caught up with each others doings for the past ten years.

My cousin is not a regular issue Christian, but as I said earlier, she is a person of real faith and courage. She could be classified as living below the poverty line. One morning she phoned me and told me that she was going up the coast to try and sell her pelicans to a gift shop owner in a big fashionable resort. So I told her I would pray that she would receive the largest order she had ever received. The following evening the telephone rang and on the other end R's excited voice told me I wouldn't believe what had happened; not only had the gift shop owner bought out her whole stock, but a gentleman who owns a chain of gift shops in a northern state had ordered as many of her works as she could make for him. She was breathless with wonder and said, "Oh Helen, my anxiety now is whether I have the ability to fill such a large order." I replied, "Of course you can R., we're like the people who pray for rain and get a cloudburst. God is showing His love for you. He wants you to be able to eat and not have to worry about where the money's coming from, so He has opened a door for you."

If only more of our unemployed had R's faith in God's love and prayer, perhaps God would open more doors for them too.

This is the story of a daughter praying for her mother.

Since my conversion experience I am one of those people, one of those ridiculous people who feel that all of their prayers have been answered. I have never felt that there was some silent emptiness when I prayed. I know that I am childlike in my faith; so maybe my lack of intellectualism has saved me from the awful feeling of unanswered prayers. I live within the heart of my Good Shepherd, His eye is forever on me, and all things are to His good purposes. This is not just a litany of faith, in my life God has evidenced Himself time after time.

When I was changed, I knew I had to forgive and pray for my mother. After twenty years of alcoholism, she was committed to a mental institution. The psychiatrists said that her situation was hopeless. Alcohol had destroyed too many of her brain cells. Eight years passed—I prayed for my mother and the doctors all said there was no hope. Then she was released to try a parole for about the sixth time. This time she met a grand man at the ballpark. He was a bachelor, eighteen years younger than she. He owned his own home, had worked for Bethlehem Steel for thirty years, and fell head over heels in love with my mother. She never again had to go back to the mental hospital, her personality changed, she was married at seventy and spent the last years of her life with a degree of happiness she had not known since my father had died.

"Intercession is the utterance of our lives, it is love on its knees."

I define intervention as a happening, mysterious, undefinable, unexpected, not governed by the laws of cause and effect, but a token of God's love and His power to answer our prayers. We modern Americans, conditioned by technological, scientific wonders, should look up and out and expect God to act supra-scientifically in answer to prayer. Hasn't our Lord Himself enjoined us to do so when He said, "If you have faith as a grain of mustard seed, ye shall say unto this mountain, be thou taken up and cast into the midst of the sea and it shall be done unto you according to your faith."

I have deliberately written here about the ordinary small interventions that happen to ordinary small people like us every day, because most of us are not famous public figures or superstars or great artists, and God's love is just as powerful towards us as it is towards the superstars.

> "But ye are a chosen generation, a royal priesthood, an holy nation, a peculiar people."
>
> I PETER 2:9

12 ⁂ THE MYSTERY OF PRAYER AND CHRISTIAN CITIZENSHIP

How is prayer related to Christian citizenship in this great land of ours—in fact, in any land where there is even a minority of Christians? Has God been mysteriously involved in the founding, the settling, the establishing of America?

It is good to remember that the Pilgrims bathed in prayer their great adventure to our wilderness continent. Here were men and women so passionately committed to the need to worship God as they felt led to worship God that they fell on their knees in prayer before they embarked on their historic voyage, commended their whole enterprise daily to God in prayer during the long and terrifying Atlantic crossing, and as they stepped out onto Plymouth Rock on that stormy November day, their first act was to fall on their knees again in praise and thanksgiving.

My own ancestor who came to Massachusetts in the early 1620's was a man of profound faith and prayer. We have the deed of sale of salt marshland in Massachusetts which he bought from an Indian chief named Serunk, and to whom he witnessed to his faith in Christ. He and his wife and thirteen children ventured down to Long Island and then New Jersey and started colonies of praying Christians in both places. He died at a ripe old age as a minister of the First Congregational Church in Sandwich, Massachusetts.

He was one of the thousands of immigrants to these shores in the 1600's and 1700's who prayed and flung their lives after their prayers, and with matchless faith and courage began to fashion the American dream which we express in our salute to the flag, "One nation, under God, with liberty and justice for all."

This dream is vividly expressed in the great seal of the United States, the inspiration for which came on the very day of the signing of the Declaration of Independence:

RESOLVED: That Dr. Franklin, Mr. J. Adams, and Mr. Jefferson be a committee to prepare a device for a Seal of the United States of North America.

It was late in the day of July 4, 1776. The Declaration of Independence had been signed earlier that afternoon. The urgency of the Resolution, and the calibre of the men selected for this first Committee, marked the significance of the Seal for the Founding Fathers. . . .

We Americans take it for granted that our country should have a Seal. Most of us carry it around in our pockets, printed on the back of every dollar bill. But how it was created, and what it says, rarely crosses our minds. . . .

It was the firm belief of the Founding Fathers that the creation of the United States had come about with divine help. . . .

Jefferson wrote in his "Notes on Virginia":

Can the liberties of a nation be thought secure when we have removed their only firm basis, a conviction in the minds of the people that those liberties are the gift of God? . . .
I tremble for my country when I reflect that God is just; that His justice cannot sleep forever.

The Great Awakening, and the thinking of such men as Jonathan Edwards, had been at work in the minds of that part of the population who actually fought the Revolutionary War. Many of them were convinced that more than "taxation without representation" was at stake in their fight with England. They had begun to see the creation of the United States of America as part of a larger plan, the coming of freedom as the key to a greater dream. . . .

What does the Great Seal say? What is the meaning of its symbols? Take a dollar bill out of your pocket and look at it. The eagle greets the exiled out of every land with the olive branch; while yet prepared for war, he holds the arrows of perpetual victory full in sight of those who tyrannize mankind. . . .

The Obverse of the Seal may be said to represent the power and strength of America. The Reverse has to do with the beliefs of the Founding Fathers as to how this nation came into being and where it was destined to go.

The philosophy of the Reverse, as well as the Obverse, was basic to the thinking of the men who founded our country. This money talks. What does it say? Is the imprint on one and one half billion dollar bills a throw-back to the past, or a target for the future?*

In a book entitled *Freedom and Faith,* Samuel Shoemaker describes the wonder of our American beginnings and the Founding Fathers' need to resort to prayer to resolve their sometimes violent differences of opinion as they struggled to write the Constitution and the Bill of Rights.

The coming together of the thirteen original colonies, and their final success in establishing themselves as the United States of America, constitutes one of the greatest achievements of all time. We were an individualistic people then, as we are individualistic now. For a time it did not look as if the union could be achieved. At the end of June 1787, the outlook was dark. Then Benjamin Franklin, who was eighty-one, rose and addressed General Washington in these lofty and inspired words: "The small progress we have made . . . our different sentiments on almost every question, several of the last producing as many Noes as Ayes is, methinks, a melancholy proof of the imperfection of the human understanding. We indeed seem to feel our want of political wisdom, since we

---

* H. Kenaston Twitchell, "The Founding Fathers Put It All Together" (Princeton: Princeton University Press). Order from Anglican Fellowship.

have been running all about in search of it. We have gone back to ancient history for models of government, and examining the different forms of those republics, which, having been formed with the seeds of their own dissolution, now no longer exist; and we have viewed modern states all around Europe, but find none of their constitutions suitable to our circumstance. In this situation of this assembly, groping as it were in the dark to find political strength, and scarce able to distinguish it when presented to us, how has it happened, Sir, that we have not hitherto once thought of humbly applying to the Father of Lights to illuminate our understandings? In the beginning of the contests with Britain, when we were sensible of danger, we had daily prayers in this room for Divine protection. Our prayers, Sir, were heard; and they were graciously answered. . . . I have lived Sir, a long time and the longer I live, the more convincing proofs I see of this truth: that God governs in the affairs of men. And if a sparrow cannot fall to the ground without His notice, is it probable that an empire can rise without His aid? I . . . believe that without His concurring aid we shall succeed in this political building no better than the builders of Babel. We shall be divided by our little partial local interests: our projects will be confounded; and we ourselves shall become a reproach, and by-word down to future ages. . . ." The Convention adjourned soon after and did not reconvene until August 6. By then contention and division had vanished; the Convention was saved and the Constitution of the United States was born.*

In 1835 Alexis de Toqueville, the distinguished Frenchman who visited our country to try and discover the mysterious source of what he considered the success of the American dream, went back to France and reported the following:

I sought for the greatness and genius of America in her commodius harbors and her ample rivers, and it was not there. I sought for the greatness and genius of America in her fertile fields and boundless forests, and it was not there. I sought for the greatness and genius of America in her rich mines and her vast world commerce, and it was not there. I sought for the greatness and genius of America in her public schools system and her institutions of learning, and it

* Samuel M. Shoemaker, *Freedom and Faith.*

was not there. I sought for the greatness and genius of America in her democratic Congress and her matchless Constitution, and it was not there. Not until I went into the churches of America and heard her pulpits flame with righteousness did I understand the secret of her genius and power. America is great because America is good: and if America ever ceases to be good, America will cease to be great.

How prophetically these conclusions of de Toqueville ring down the years when we consider our history—"America is great because America is good; and if America ceases to be good, America will cease to be great."

Abraham Lincoln, who was surely chosen by God to symbolize the mighty words of the Great Seal, "E Pluribus Unum," during the most dangerous threat to this Union, tells us simply, "I talk to God, my mind seems relieved when I do and a way is suggested. I should be a self-conceited blockhead if I should hope to get along without the wisdom that comes from God and not from man."

I can imagine Abraham Lincoln down on his knees in prayer as he wrote his Gettysburg address in that tiny corner room in that tiny town square in Gettysburg, and likewise down on his knees in prayer in what was then the Oval Office of the White House when he wrote his immortal second inaugural speech.

Every single American enjoys the privilege of this heritage that has been handed down to us through the blood, sweat and tears of our Founding Fathers, and through the blood, sweat, tears and prayers of millions of us ordinary citizens, mothers, wives, fathers, husbands, sons and daughters, through the 200 years of our history. A recent Gallup Poll lists the United States as the most religious of all the Western nations. Why? Because at least 100,000,000 of us have learned how to pray and are praying now that this last great hope of earth, in spite of turbulence, subversion, crime, the breakup of the family, shall not perish from the earth and that his "Amazing Grace" will renew and save us.

In other words, as I said earlier, we can pray and hurl our lives after our prayers. That is Christian Citizenship activism at its best—and God will open the doors so that He can use us in His divine plan for our nation.

There is much evil in this nation.

Syphilis and gonorrhea are at an all-time high because of a wrong understanding of what unbridled sex can do to destroy our bodies. Pray and see if you are led to act in regard to this.

Pornography is rampant. Are you attacking it in your communities for it debases the mind of the young? Pray and see if you are led to act.

There is corruption in business and government. All the evil in the country was not centered in Watergate.

Freedom of the press and the news media, unless it polices itself, can be used to dangerously manipulate our thinking and action, especially the thinking and acting of impressionable young people. Pray about this.

Do you ask God to show you how you can act to keep America good and consequently great?

You can pray and write to your newspapers.

You can pray and work to elect honest officials.

You can pray and call a halt to unbridled sexual immorality and indulgence.

You can begin thinking through the reasons for so much divorce and challenge this trend.

You can concern yourself with the old, poor, the young, the unemployed and the too often neglected veterans. You can concern yourself with the terrible state of our prisons, how to deal with crime in the streets, violence in our schools, veneral disease and drugs. I could go on and on. Each of us can do something and above all we can pray, pray, pray.

One group in Washington calling itself the United Prayer Force has circulated a small card which calls us to daily prayer for the following needs:

THE UNITED PRAYER FORCE

11 A.M. Prayer Break
Daily Prayer Reminder

For our nation and one another

II Chronicles 7:14

Join with the thousands who are already praying
daily at 11 A.M.

SUNDAY—PRAY FOR GOD'S MERCY AND FORGIVE-
NESS
Asking God . . .
(1) to pierce our apathy and indifference
(2) for a contrite heart and spiritual renewal
(3) recommitting ourselves to:
Study His word
Pray steadfastly
Seek His will and strength to accomplish His
purposes
I John 1:9

MONDAY—PRAY FOR THE LEADERS OF OUR
COUNTRY
That they might have wisdom, guidance, integ-
rity, courage, protection, and awareness of
God's presence in mind and heart:

President	Cabinet
Vice President	Congress
Presidential advisors	Supreme Court

Ambassadors and all others in places of authority
here and abroad.
I Timothy 2:1–6   Jeremiah 33:3

TUESDAY—PRAY FOR THE LEADERS OF OUR CITY,
COUNTY AND STATE

| Mayor | Governor |
| City Officials | Lt. Governor |

County officials	State Legislators
Courts, School Boards,	Educators, Civic
Committeemen	Employees
Psalm 127:1	

WEDNESDAY—PRAY FOR THE ENLARGEMENT OF GOD'S KINGDOM AND HIS PEACE

For God's Holy Word and its understanding to be increased mightily;

A Spirit-filled life, equipping us with the whole armor of God;

Unity within the Body of Christ;

Translation and literacy efforts to be intensified

| John 3:16 | John 14:27 |

THURSDAY—PRAY FOR OUR NATION

Thanksgiving and gratitude for God's blessings, and for living in this great country that was founded in God's name.

For all those who have gone before us providing the freedom we now enjoy.

Asking God:

To awaken us to a spirit of responsibility in behalf of our nation.

For His intervention in all areas of government, in mass media, labor and industry, science, research, medicine, education, prisons, court systems and the welfare of us all.

For His touch upon those who are a burden to our nation imprisoned by drugs, alcohol, immorality, pornography, crime, prejudice, unbelief and despair

Psalm 33

FRIDAY—PRAY FOR ONE ANOTHER*

Purification of our thoughts and deeds, that we

* "Cooperating with the Church at Large, Fasting and Praying for our Nation on the first Friday of every month." United Prayer Force, Inc. P.O. Box 30289, Washington, D.C. 20014.

may be fit instruments and channels for God's
love.

We bring before Thee our loved ones, friends,
neighbors, those who serve us in all walks of
life, the unloving (to us), those in adversity,
our people in the military, unbelievers, our
enemies, others and ourselves.

By God's outpouring spirit, to be empowered
people witnessing His great love by word and
deed to one another.

James 5:16   I John 4:7–21

What is so mysterious about prayer and the birth and
growth and preservation of a nation? Consider the record and
ask yourself these questions.

Was prayer important to the Pilgrim Fathers?

Did Prayer permeate the Great Awakening of the early
1700's?

Did God's mysterious design for America bring some extraordinary men to the leadership of this nation, men such as
Washington, Jefferson, Adams and Franklin in 1775?

Did prayer influence the writing of the United States Constitution and the uniting of the thirteen colonies?

What place has prayer had in keeping this nation together
and moving forward during the 200 years of our violent and
spectacular history?

Do we still need the prayers of millions of God-fearing citizens?

Is Prayer perhaps the great underground river flowing secretly below the surface of this nation cleansing it and purifying it and purging it of its impurities?

Is this river being constantly fed by the rivulets of prayer
flowing into it by the millions of us who pray?

Is prayer the most mysterious and powerful force in the life
of this people and this nation?

"For we wrestle not against flesh and blood, but against principalities, against powers, against the rulers of the darkness of this world, against spiritual wickedness in high places."

EPHESIANS 6:12

"For our fight is not against human foes, but against cosmic powers, against the authorities and potentates of this dark world, against the super human forces of evil in the heavens. . . . To this end keep watch and persevere always interceding for all God's people."

EPHESIANS 6:12, 18
(NEW ENGLISH BIBLE)

13 ✦ THE MYSTERY OF PRAYER CHANGING THE DIRECTION OF NATIONS

NOTHING much is said or read in our news media about the place of the spiritual, the place of God and His will and His way in the current terrifying clash of world forces. We hear a lot about governments in thunderous transition, about little evil men seizing power everywhere and terrorizing hundreds of millions of people. We hear a lot of the dangers of nuclear holocaust. We have been both edified and terrified by the prophetic words of Alexander Solzhenitsyn, and those of us who believe in prayer feel that our great transcendent God in Christ will have the last word in all these frightening manifestations. How does it happen, for instance, that there is a resurgence of interest in the profoundly ancient and mysterious methods of the great Indian gurus who plumb through to the heart of the energies throbbing through the universe? How does it happen that an Alexander Solzhenitsyn should have appeared on the scene so unexpectedly and so powerfully right now? How does it happen that, in the midst of the turmoil, in the midst of the frightening cruelty and vicious violence of terrorists, gangsters and slaughterers of all kinds, there is also a cloud of hope on the horizon— millions in Africa turning to Christ as their savior; millions in Indonesia, in South Korea, in South America; millions finding a renewal of their faith through various ministries of the Spirit; great, creative, spiritual pronouncements from great, creative councils of the Church in Rome, and great, creative prophets in our American Church. Where does the newly awakened concern over hunger and oppression come from? Isn't it the result of the secret rivulet of prayer being poured in by millions of people like you and me all over the world; people who are constantly, consciously, praying in response to our Lord's example and command for a new revelation of His healing and His power? So as we are told so movingly in the Epistle to the Hebrews, "Lift up the hands, which hang down, and the feeble knees" (Hebrews 12:12). Realize again that "if God be for you, who can be against you? He that spared not His own Son but delivered Him up for us all— shall He not also freely give us all things?" Prayer has influenced the direction of nations before in history; it can influence it again now.

In the early nineteenth century in England, as she was moving into an era of great prosperity and preeminence in world trade and colonial expansion, one lonely man arose in parliament and began pointing to the evils of the slave trade on which some of England's Colonial prosperity rested. His name was William Wilberforce, the eldest son of a family from Hull which dated its lineage back to the era of Henry the Second. He was born in 1759 and died in 1833. After a rather irresponsible youth, he became a friend of William Pitt, ran for Parliament from Hull and won in 1783. He came under the influence of the Dean of Carlisle, a leading evangelical, and was born again in 1758. He met Thomas Clarkson and began to agitate against the slave trade which made him extremely unpopular with very powerful slave traders out of Bristol who stood to lose 6,000,000 pounds per year should he succeed in inducing Parliament to abolish it. It is told that he met regularly for prayer with four friends and was given the courage to persist. Lord Shaftsbury joined him in the House of Lords and, supported by the prayers of their friends, the Emancipation Bill, after searing political battles, was finally passed one year after his death in 1833. There were worldwide repercussions; like a stone thrown into a pool, the ripples spread and spread and spread and are still spreading. One man, two men, six men, pounding on the gates of heaven without ceasing and accomplishing John Wesley's prophecy—''God will do nothing on earth except in answer to believing prayers.''

We in America are so committed to proving everything by a pragmatic, scientific yardstick that we've almost lost the capacity to wonder before the mysterious forces that are brought into play by strong, united, unceasing prayer. Recently a book has come to my attention by Jack Hayford, pastor of the Church On the Way in Van Nuys, California. The title of his book is compelling: *Prayer Is Invading the Impossible*. It promptly took my mind back to another book which I read some years ago which described a group of Welsh Christians who, during World War II, banded together to pray daily that the world would be delivered from the menace of Hitler. They prayed either that God would overthrow him or that deliverance would come in some other way. This was a powerful daily commitment for these people, and it is a strange and mysterious thing that, while we didn't know it at the time, the German war code was stolen and decoded by the British (which has been powerfully described in the book, *A Man Called Intrepid,* and another book, *The Ultra Secret*), so that the allies were aware ahead of time of Hitler's whole strategy and were able to thwart his strategy, until the final cataclysm when Hitler took his own life in a bunker in Berlin and the free world was delivered from him. It was a frightful struggle, but these Welsh prayers believed that God had called them to pit the forces of light against the forces of darkness and that they were to pray constantly and specifically that the forces of light would prevail. Many pragmatic secularists and scientists would pooh-pooh this, but there is a mysterious net of circumstances here that nobody can pooh-pooh.

In 1857 America was in the depths of despair and darkness. War was threatening. Slavery cut the nation to the bone. America was gripped in a continuing economic and spiritual crisis. One man, Jeremiah Lamphier, invited *five* businessmen to join him in a weekly prayer session. The crisis deepened. The men began to meet daily. Within six months 10,000 people were gathering in the streets of New York as the noon bells tolled to repent and pray for America. From this seemingly insignificant beginning one of the greatest awakenings of modern times swept the Western world; the spirit of a nation was strengthened to endure the Civil War and then to be raised to new heights of greatness.*

Take your tiny seed of faith and plant it in the ground of God's love and concern for the world, water it with your

* Charles W. Colson, *Born Again* (Old Tappan, N.J.: Fleming Revell, 1976).

prayers and imagine it joined to the millions of other tiny seeds of faith planted by European and African, South American, and Asian Christians scattered on all the islands of the seas, and you may see in your lifetime a glory of faith and hope and freedom that only He can give in response.

God wants to repossess His world. He is repossessing it through our prayers. We are engaged in warfare for the peace of the world, the liberation of the world, from the power of Satan, the destroyer of human life and freedom, "the principalities and powers, the rulers of darkness of this world." Our only weapon, yet the most powerful weapon of all, is ceaseless, relentless, redemptive prayer.

> *There is a shock wave more unsettling*
>   *Than an earthquake*
> *More irresistible*
>   *Than a tidal wave*
> *More uncontrollable than a tornado*
> *But a thousand times more desirable*
>   *Than any of them.* *

---

*Jack W. Hayford, *Prayer is Invading the Impossible* (Plainfield, N.J.: Logos International).

"Neither pray I for these alone, but for them also which shall believe on me through their word; That they all may be one; as thou, Father, art in me, and I in thee, that they also may be one in us: that the world may believe that thou hast sent me."

ST. JOHN 17:20–21

14 ✷ THE MYSTERY OF PRAYER UNITES

PRAYER is indeed communication with mystery. It unites us with our Lord and Savior, as well as with each other. When I say each other, I mean two people coming from very different lifestyles, different ages, different social orientations, different political views, different attitudes on all public questions of Church and state, different denominations. Is anything more needed in today's world than this thrilling fact that, when people as disparate as the members of Christ's Church can kneel together in prayer or attend the sacrament together, they find, as John Wesley once put it so clearly, "their spirits are strangely warmed," and they are drawn into the kind of fellowship in our Lord for which He prayed in the great high priestly prayer of John 17, "That they all may be one in us; that the world may believe that Thou has sent me"?

The Anglican Fellowship of Prayer has taken the theme

"Prayer Unites" because a very rich and wonderful uniting took place in our own fellowship at the time of one of our great church conventions several years ago. At that time the matter of race was before us and we were very deeply divided in the Church as to how to handle it.

The Holy Spirit led the Anglican Fellowship of Prayer to unite with the Daughters of the King and the Order of Saint Luke in the exhibition area under a great banner on which was printed in brilliant felt letters, "Fellowship in Prayer." At this particular convention a wonderful layman from Detroit conceived and produced for us 3,000 yellow buttons with "Prayer Unites" written in black letters on them. He personally brought them to the convention and was present when the doors opened every morning so that he might give the bishops and deputies a button for their lapels as they came into the convention hall. We also held a breakfast each morning for those of us who were members of our fellowship team, and we established a hot line to our home dioceses. One of us was always present in the House of Bishops and the House of Deputies in prayer while the debate raged.

So far so good; but to our consternation we discovered that we in our own fellowship rather violently disagreed about racism. I had joined a group called "Episcopalians for Responsible Social Action" and some of our American Fellowship of Prayer members disapproved of my action. One of us felt strongly that a prayer fellowship had no business getting involved in social legislation. Others felt that we had to challenge the whole idea of racism. One morning it all boiled over at our breakfast and all of our feelings of frustration, anger, hostility, and disagreement erupted at the dining room table—until a father of the Order of the Holy Cross, who was breakfasting with us, mildly suggested that as our motto was "Prayer Unites" we might practice that philosophy. So we prayed and as we prayed the hostility and the anger and the frustration were all drained away, and we were able to free one another to be and do and say the thing we felt led to be and do and say. A great love for each other flowed into us and, while we continued to disagree about how the Church might resolve this explosive issue, we in our fellowship knew that we could pray together in unity and power in spite of political differences of opinion.

And then things began to happen: the Father Superior of the Order of the Holy Cross wished to join us and we began to lay the foundations of what later became known as "Pewsaction." Pewsaction now includes seventeen different ministries in our Church. When the Presiding Bishop was searching for a task force to support him in prayer as he prepared to come to grips with the seriously divisive issues coming before the General Convention of 1976 (the ordination of women and Prayer Book revision), he turned to the Department of Evangelism and Renewal and the leaders of Pewsaction to help him prepare a conference telephone call including all the twenty-eight ministries in the Church. These ministries, as disparate as "the Foundation for Christian Theology," the Women's Caucus, the Black Caucus, and the Society for the Preservation of the Book of Common Prayer, were to agree to pray constantly that the Holy Spirit might be present at General Convention to calm our spirits and unite our hearts in love and compassion and respect for one another, no matter which way the voting went. And in a mysterious and miraculous way this did happen.

Now in 1977 the Presiding Bishop is again calling us to united prayer, because like Christ and His disciples who had to come down off the mountain of transfiguration to meet a valley full of confused and unhappy people, there is tremendous need for the healing and uniting and renewing and reconciling power of prayer to continue in our dioceses. Can anything else so effectively support our bishops and lay persons in our dioceses and parishes in these tormenting days?

As I have said elsewhere, the forces of evil seem to be tearing our nation and our world apart and yet God in His mysterious mercy is highlighting for us great symbols of reconciliation, in answer to the prayers of millions of citizens. The other day I was sent a clipping from the *Washington Post* containing a picture of two of the most recently notorious sinners on the national scene, apparently reconciled in Christ. The newspaper article read as follows:

RELIGION UNITES TWO "ENEMIES" *

There they were yesterday, former black militant leader Eldridge Cleaver and former Nixon White House political operative Charles Colson, embracing and talking about their newfound brotherly love. Once poles apart politically, Colson and Cleaver who both now profess to be "born again" Christians, have been making joint appearances since meeting last August.

"I just want to surround him and love him as a brother," Colson said of Cleaver at a press conference of religious broadcasters yesterday. "I think God has raised him up to do marvelous things."

Cleaver, who is awaiting trial on charges of attempted murder in a 1968 shootout with police, described Colson as an understanding person, someone who walks in the same shoes.

"He can understand what I'm going through because he's an old convict," said Cleaver, grinning.

Cleaver has indicated that his conversion began in the South of France in 1975 when he was feeling low. He was watching the sky and began to see faces in the moon, faces of his old heroes—Fidel Castro and Mao Tse-tung. Then the face turned to Jesus. He said he began to cry uncontrollably.

Cleaver said he began praying and reading the Bible regularly. About a year ago, after his return to the United States after seven years in exile, he became a Christian while in the Alameda County Jail in Oakland, Calif. . . .

"Since this has happened to me, I haven't met one person I don't love," he said yesterday.

Colson's conversion was widely publicized in 1974 and recounted in his best selling book, *Born Again*. His main work now is teaching prison inmates about Christ.

*Reprinted by permission of *The Washington Post,* © The Washington Post.

Colson said yesterday, "I'm not the author of the (Nixon White House) enemies list, although everyone thinks I am, but had I been, I would have put him (Cleaver) as Public Enemy No. 1. To me he was a radical Marxist-Leninist militant bomb-thrower."

As for Cleaver's earlier view of Colson, "He was Nixon's hatchet man and therefore my enemy. I had contempt for him. I was glad when he got arrested and exposed. . . . When I was in jail, someone gave me his book and I put it on the shelf. I kept it there for several months. One day I picked it up and was immediately fascinated with the verse about the metamorphosis of a butterfly. . . . Now I love him as my brother in Christ," Cleaver declared.

"I don't like the Christian exhibitionism, the carnival-like atmosphere of taking a couple of celebrities like Cleaver and Colson," said Colson. "But I feel deeply that what we symbolize is the reconciling power of Christ."

But Colson's most spectacular illustration of "prayer unites" is the times he describes praying in depth with a former Grand Kleagle of the Ku Klux Klan from Mississippi, now a "lifer" in the state prison for bombing the homes of blacks and Jews; Harold Hughes, a former U. S. Senator, a dove and a democrat; Eldridge Cleaver; and himself—what a mysterious thing that four men of such totally opposite backgrounds and mind-sets, can be brought together through a common loyalty to Jesus Christ so that prayer in His name can reconcile their spirits and lift them to a type of unity and understanding that is humanly impossible but spiritually natural.

Another symbol of the reconciling power of Christ has taken place in our nation recently as two praying Christian men, a former president of the United States and a newly elected president of the United States, managed a transfer of power so filled with generosity, Christian consideration and Christian understanding that as an average citizen I was proud to be an American and proud of our witness to the world. In practically no nation has the transfer of power been accomplished with so little acrimony and hostility, not to mention violence. Could this, too, be the mysterious result of our millions of small prayers?

There is not time to mention how prayer unites us with ourselves as well as with God, or how prayer unites two married people who have been drifting apart or parents and children whose relationship has been shattered. In fact, the mysterious unifying aspect of prayer may ultimately prove to be important to man's final destiny. Is any other force as powerful in the whole universe of God?

"Who maketh his angels spirits and his ministers a flame of fire."

HEBREWS 1:7

"The Empire of Angels is as vast as God's Creation."

BILLY GRAHAM, Angels

"Angels are the Princes of Heaven who stand before God."

BILLY GRAHAM, Angels

15 * THE MYSTERY OF THE MINISTRY OF ANGELS

THE Bible is full of references to angels. The Bible teaches that a guardian angel watches over each human being born into the world, and yet we so seldom hear of this from the pulpit. The Orthodox Church, at the baptism of an infant, gives this child a guardian angel to watch over him throughout life; this is a prime part of Orthodox faith.

Who are these mysterious flashing beings?

According to Billy Graham:

The empire of angels is as vast as God's creation. If you believe the Bible, you will believe in their ministry. They crisscross the Old and New Testaments, being mentioned directly and indirectly nearly 300 times. As to their number, David recorded 20,000, even thousands of angels.'' *

In the Book of Revelations and in the Gospel narratives we are told of legions of angels. There were hosts of angels at our Lord's nativity, and legions of angels who could have come to His rescue if He had called upon them to protect Him before His crucifixion.

Angels are the princes of heaven who stand before God. They are also ministering spirits to those who are heirs of salvation. Angels are of a different order than human beings, although they closely resemble human appearance; the angels are spirit beings but not disembodied spirits. They have bodies, though not physical bodies, yet they have power to appear as physical beings at such times as they choose. On occasion, they may show themselves in their full heavenly glory. Usually they appear to people in such a form as not to overawe those whom they visit. They take on human form and may be mistaken for men. They are of a higher order than man in his present state. There are different orders of angels, including seraphim, cherubim, archangels, and guardian angels. The seraphim are described as having three pairs of wings. They are attendants of the Lord and have special duties, proclaiming the holiness of the Lord. The cherubim have two pairs of wings and have certain responsibility in guarding the throne of God.

Angels are spoken of in the masculine gender, although we are specifically informed that they do not marry nor are given in marriage. They are immortal and do not die.

The activity of angels is ceaseless. Angels are watching over all believers protecting them from unseen dangers and evil.

Ordinarily, when angels appear to men, they at once deliver their message, then with equal celerity, depart. Righteous angels worship God and will not receive worship directly to themselves. Angels possess a superior intelligence. Angels, however, do not possess omniscience.

* Billy Graham, *Angels: God's Secret Agents*, (New York: Doubleday, 1975), p. 19.

The movement of angels is marvelous. In a single instant an angel comes from heaven to earth and goes from one end of the universe to the other without passing through intermediate space. To understand the angelic movement, we have only to compare them with thought. In a moment, our thought passes from heaven to earth, from England to China, from end to end of the earth.

Although angels are exceedingly powerful as compared with men, they more nearly meet their match in combating the evil angels which follow Satan. In their conflicts with them they must depend on God for victory. When Satan fully mobilizes his hosts, he may command such power as requires as many as twelve legions of angels to overcome it.*

The Bible speaks of three great archangels by name. However, in the Apocrypha in the Book of Esdras, and in other great Christian traditions, there are seven archangels mentioned. For instance, the Coptic Church mentions Michael, Raphael, Sadakel, Ananiel, Gabriel, Suriel and Saraphael. According to research done by Massey Shephard, Jr. from a German encyclopedia on angels, entitled *Engel Reallexicon Antivue und Christentum,* Vol. 5, by Johann Michl and Theodor Vlauser, the Suriel mentioned in the Coptic tradition often occurs in place of Uriel, and he strongly suspects that Uriel and Suriel are one and the same. This is strengthened by the fact that in the Dead Sea Scrolls document known as the "War Scrolls" 1015–16, four archangels are named (Michael, Gabriel, Suriel and Raphael). It must be the same four, Uriel being called Suriel by the Coptics. We can imagine that the great archangels were leading the heavenly host in the glorious singing on the night of Jesus' birth.

Lucifer is the fallen angel. Through rebellion, he and the angels that followed him fell from heaven. In the eternal conflict between light and darkness, it seems that Lucifer, the former son of the morning, heads the forces of darkness

---

*Gordon Lindsay, *The Ministry of Angels* (Dallas: Christ for the Nations, Inc.).

against the forces of light, which are captained by the great archangel Michael.

"When will this great battle in the heavenlies be ended?" Revelation 12:8–12 gives the answer. Michael and his angels will come forth and fight against Satan, and the latter and his fallen angels will together be cast out of their positions in the heavenlies and forced down to earth where they will be permitted to continue their operations for the little season during the Great Tribulation. Although Michael and the angels are the celestial agents in the defeat and casting down of the devil and his hosts, it is interesting to note the words: "And they overcame him by the blood of the Lamb and the word of their testimony." This shows that angels alone are not the ones who effect the defeat of the devil, but it is the prayers, the faith, the testimony of the righteous who, abiding under the protection of the blood of the Lamb, also play a vital role in the overthrow of the powers of darkness.

And so as the inhabitants of the earth move rapidly toward the time of the Great Tribulation days, God is calling for men and women who will be prayer warriors in this great battle of the ages. Unceasingly, then, let God's people contend in a mighty united prayer for the defeat and dislodgement of this prince of the power of the air. When the victory comes, as it surely will, they may share the glory of having an important part in his defeat.

There is another mission performed by these invisible messengers of God. For those who have fully consecrated their lives to God, there is special angelic protection. This promise is not for all; it is for "him that dwelleth in the secret place of the Most High, who abides under the shadow of the Almighty" (Psalm 91).

Here is a promise of protection over evil, over the plague, over accident, over the power of the evil one. And later in the same Psalm we are assured that "He will give his angels charge over thee to keep thee in all thy ways; then bear thee up in their hands lest thou dash thy foot against a stone."*

What comfort and assurance this should give to us mortals as we pass through the joys and sorrows, the pitfalls and challenges and crises of our lives—and what support this witness gives us of God's infinite love.

So look up the reference to angels in your Bible and you will be amazed to read of the mighty and reassuring activities of the angels whom God sends to protect us, to guide us, to reveal God's glory to us, to heal us. During the night, morning, and often the day, I ask my Lord to send St. Michael, the Captain of the Lord's Host, the Prince of angels, to watch over those for whom I am praying that day. I ask my Lord to send St. Gabriel, the great messenger angel, to bring them God's messages. I ask My Lord to send St. Uriel, the great Shekinah angel, the angel of glory and light and wisdom, to reveal God's glory to them. And I ask my Lord to send St. Raphael to guide and keep those who travel and heal them of their sicknesses of mind and body and soul.

And Last of all, I will ask my Lord for those who are dying and for myself when my time comes to die, that He will send His Holy Angels to gather us up and carry us into His living presence, so that we may dwell with Him forever.

The words from a beautiful hymn sum it up:

> *Angels and ministers, spirits of grace.*
> *Friends of the children, beholding God's face,*
> *Moving like thought to us through the beyond,*
> *Molded in beauty, and free from our bond!*

> *Messengers clad in the swiftness of light,*
> *Subtle as flame, and creative in might,*
> *Helmed with the truth and with charity shod,*
> *Wielding the wind of the purpose of God!*

---

* Gordon Lindsay, *ibid.*

"But unto every one of us is given grace
according to the measure of the gift of
Christ. . . . And he gave some, apostles;
and some, prophets; and some, evangelists;
and some, pastors and teachers; For the perfecting of the saints, for the work of the
ministry, for the edifying of the body of
Christ. Till we all come in the unity of the
faith, and of the knowledge of the Son of
God, unto a perfect man, unto the measure
of the stature of the fulness of Christ."

EPHESIANS 4:7, 11–13

✻✻✻✻✻✻✻✻✻✻✻✻✻✻✻✻✻✻✻✻✻✻✻✻✻✻

16 ✻ THE MYSTERY OF GRACE AND GIFTS

ST. THOMAS AQUINAS, the great Catholic theologian,
tells us, "Grace is nothing else than a kind of beginning of
glory in us."

Recently I heard a sermon preached by an old, frail and
holy Anglican bishop in which the glory was shining. He
said he wanted to talk to us about two women, Eve and
Mary. Eve, the first woman, created in perfection and
beauty, was given a choice. God said to her, "In the garden
where I have placed you, there is a tree, and on that tree
there is a fruit. You shall not eat of that fruit or you will
die."

Eve was intrigued and curious, and at that point a green serpent slid towards her and said, "Eat of the fruit for God knows that on the day you eat it, you and your husband will become gods and know good and evil." So in her pride and ambition she disobeyed God and ate the fruit and God drove her and her husband out of the garden to experience all the vicissitudes of life which we have all experienced ever since.

Ages later God sent the angel Gabriel to a young girl, Mary, as she was kneeling in prayer. St. Luke tells us, "And the angel came in unto her and said, 'Hail Thou art highly favored, the Lord is with Thee, blessed art Thou among women. Behold Thou shalt conceive in thy womb, and bring forth a son and shall call His name Jesus, and He shall be great and shall be called the Son of the Highest.' And Mary replied in sublime humility and obedience, 'Behold, the handmaid of the Lord, be it with me according to Thy word.' "

Two women, Eve and Mary, each given the choice of obedience, one disobeyed, becoming the first mother of sinful humanity; the other obeyed and became the mother of God.

We are all asked to choose who we will listen to, to the voice of the world, the voice of the evil one, or the voice of God. And if we listen to the voice of God and obey we are given the grace to win.

This saintly old bishop is an illustration of St. Paul's saying, "My grace is sufficient for you, for my strength is made perfect in weakness, therefore will I rather glory in mine infirmities that the power of Christ may rest upon me." Here before our eyes was a man, old, frail, with a weak wispy voice who had obeyed the voice of God and gone to Burma many years ago as a missionary. The grace of glory began there for him. He tells of visiting an island where the native people were so primitive that they wore only a loincloth. A native born-again Christian had been there before him, and consequently 700 of these men and women had been won to Christ, but like the new Christians in the book of Acts they had not yet received the gift of the spirit through baptism and the laying on of hands. When the bishop arrived they greeted him like an angel and begged him to lay his hands on them. He says that he felt utterly humanly unequal to the challenge, so he knelt in prayer, and received first a new infusion of the gift of the Spirit himself so that when he did lay his hands on the people the thing happened that Jesus had promised—"Ye shall be baptized with the Holy Spirit and with fire."

This bishop has been tested in life down through the years; his health gave way, a serious infection robbed him of his voice so that he was forced to retire from his bishopric. No ill health, no vicissitudes have been able to rob him of the grace of victory, and when he blessed us at the close of the service, we knew what the blessing fully meant. "The Grace of the Lord Jesus Christ and the love of God and the fellowship of the Holy Spirit be with you and remain with you always." We went from that church refreshed and renewed by the grace streaming through one tired, frail, old man who had obeyed God's voice throughout his life and won. "Grace is nothing else than a kind of beginning of God's glory in us."

It is clearly told us in the New Testament that God's grace is given to us; we can't earn it, it issues in various gifts which enable us to witness to His resurrection power.

The overall gift is the gift of the Holy Spirit, His Living Spirit, which Jesus promised would come to comfort us, guide us, interpret His will to us, empower us. This gift came in abundance to the disciples at Pentecost, as they obeyed Jesus' command to wait together in prayer, in unity of spirit and expectancy. It came like a hurricane, it came in tongues of fire. It gave them the ability to speak in their own language to the huge crowd of needy Jews gathered in Jerusalem from every land under the sun, to speak of Jesus and His resurrection.

Later St. Paul tells us that there are varieties of gifts which God has in His power to give us. St. Paul's first letter to the Corinthians, chapter twelve, says the various gifts are compared to the various parts of the body, all necessary to a whole healthy body. In his letter to the Ephesians, St. Paul sweeps it all together when He says, "One Lord, one faith, one baptism, One God and Father of all, who is above all, and through all, and in you all. But unto every one of us is given grace according to the measure of the gift of Christ. And he gave some, apostles; and some, prophets; and some, evangelists; and some, pastors and teachers; For the perfecting of the saints, for the work of the ministry, for the edifying of the body of Christ: Till we all come in the unity of the faith, and of the knowledge of the Son of God, unto a perfect man, unto the measure of the stature of the fullness of Christ" (Ephesians 4:5–13).

Here he tells of the mysterious wonder of it all when he speaks of the gift of Christ. This is something we do not work or struggle for. It is the reward of our faith in Christ, our obedience to Him and our love for Him. It is given from Christ Himself. To some of us He gives the gift of apostleship, to some the gift of prophecy, to some the gift of evangelism, to some the gift of pastoring, to some the gift of teaching. It is all for one glorious purpose that we whom He has called and chosen might become polished instruments for His use so that we may edify and unite others.

This beginning of glory in us is what Jesus meant in the mysterious statement, "Be ye therefore perfect as your Father in Heaven is perfect." I have always had great trouble with this statement and I've asked that God would interpret to me what Jesus meant by it. The other day I got my answer. I was reading a small sheet by Richard Halverson called "Perspective"; in it he says, "Perfection is not so much a goal as it is a relationship." All of a sudden I understood as I had never understood before what the great blessing of the

Church means: "The Grace of our Lord Jesus Christ, the love of God and the Fellowship of the Holy Spirit" is the beginning of glory in us.

Does this glorious blessing give you the same sense of high and worthwhile adventuring as it does me? Because you can have it; His grace will sustain you in your discouraged times, your doubting times, your afraid times, your weak times, for as St. Thomas Aquinas says, "Grace is nothing else than a kind of beginning of glory in us" and as we move forward in that glory, He shows us gifts we didn't even know we had and then gives us the grace to use them for His glory.

Ask Him to show you your gift or gifts and then show you how to use them for His glory. He will.

If you feel pedestrian and unimportant remember what Brother Lawrence, that Renaissance monk who spent his whole adult life amid the pots and pans of a monastery kitchen tells us: "When God finds a soul penetrated with a living faith, He pours into it His graces and favors plentifully; there they flow like a torrent which spreads itself with impetuosity and abundance." *

---

* Brother Lawrence, *The Practice of the Presence of God,* Forward Movement Publications.

"Do ye not know that the saints shall judge the world?"

I CORINTHIANS 6:2

꙾⳼⳼⳼⳼⳼⳼⳼⳼⳼⳼⳼⳼⳼⳼⳼⳼⳼⳼⳼⳼⳼⳼⳼⳼꙾

17 ⳾ THE MYSTERY OF THE CHURCH ALIVE

THE foundation rock of the Church of Christ (whose body we are) is the mysterious word of St. Peter, when he said in a glorious flash of insight, "Thou art the Christ, the Son of the Living God," and Jesus' mysterious reply, "On this rock, Peter [that is the rock of your faith] I will build my church and the gates of hell shall not prevail against it."

A little later Jesus says trustingly and tenderly to His twelve apostles as He walks to Jerusalem to His death and resurrection, "Fear not, little flock, it is my Father's good pleasure to give you the kingdom."

Jesus reinforced these two promises with one other when He said to the disciples, in the eighth verse of the first chapter of the Book of Acts, "But ye shall receive power, after that the Holy Ghost has come upon you; and ye shall be witnesses unto me both in Jerusalem, and in all Judea, and in Samaria, and unto the uttermost parts of the earth." With these words He ascended into heaven and the joyous disciples literally obeying His command retired together to the upper room in Jerusalsm where we are told they waited in unity of spirit and in prayer for the promise of His Holy Spirit which was, as we all know, swept through them with such power that it sounded like a rushing mighty wind and tongues of fire sat upon all their heads. From that upper room they streamed into the pagan world and nothing has been able to stop them because, through the centuries whenever the flame of faith began to die down, other upper rooms in other parts of the then known world took place. Men and women went to their knees in prayer in unity of spirit and the Holy Spirit with wind and flame re-invigorated, re-empowered, re-infused them with the wonder and the mystery of the person of Christ.

On these three mighty and mysterious promises, like three pillars of a temple, are built the Christian Church which has experienced for 2,000 years the wonderful truth of them, in spite of retreats, apostasy, heresy, betrayal, fallings away, sweepings away by pagan world forces, persecution, torture, death, murder, martyrdom, apathy; the flame of faith in our Lord Jesus Christ, which is the heart of the Church Alive, is today strangely and mysteriously burning more brightly than ever.

In the introduction to a most remarkable little book entitled *Celtic Sunrise,** George McCleod, the modern saint and prophet of the reconstructed Iona community, writes:

St. Peter and St. John were true disciples of our Lord, who forever point us both to a narrow gate and to wide horizons. Both can be in the direction of the sunrise. St. Peter, with his keys, consumed with the problem of the gate. St. John, of the mountain top, was entranced with the nearness of the land which was very far off. It is no accident that the last remaining relic of the Celtic Church on Iona is St. John's cross standing just outside the Roman period abbey, at the laying of whose earliest foundation stone, that cross by then already old, stood sentinal. Nor is it an accident that St.

---

*Dianna Leatham, *Celtic Sunrise* (London: Hodder & Stoughton).

John was the patron saint of Scotland for centuries before the Roman dominance placed in his stead St. Andrew. Least of all perhaps was it an accident that this same cross was smashed to smithereens. The keys demolished it.

The modern mind, unused to personal symbols, labels the same issue as the tension between the institutional and the organic.

Perhaps as George McCleod has so graphically described it, this is the key to the mystery of the Church Alive. Through history, there is continually the tension between the institutional and the organic, and both are needed as we look back into the history of the Church. There had to be a way to bring order out of the glorious chaos of the daily witnesses to our Lord Jesus Christ's resurrection as they streamed across the pagan world and won thousands of people to a living faith in Him. There had to be order brought out of all this living, flaming, individualistic faith and commitment. And yet there always has been a need not to quench the spirit, and so often it has been in great danger of being quenched by overzealous organizers and church bureaucrats.

I'd like to take the early Christians from the first century and trace the extraordinary impact the thousands of Christian martyrs had on the pagan world. There was one time in the early centuries when all Christian children were trained to know what they should do and say if they were brought before the authorities for their faith and shown how to stand for that faith with courage and joy. When they were tortured, when they were thrown to the lions, when they were "torn asunder" as the gruesome phrase expresses it, when they were crucified, when they were burned alive, these young Christians went singing and praying into the arms of their Lord. In a later period, young Christians by the thousands went out into the desert places to be alone with their Lord so that they might receive the flaming insights that are only given to the great contemplative followers of St. John, out of whose heart and soul came the glory of the Book of Revelation. We read of St. Anthony of the Desert and the other ascetic desert fathers; we read of the great self-denying ascetics of the early Irish Church coming out of the Irish and Scotch monasteries of Bangor Clonard and Lindisfarne, Lisieux and Mt. Saint Michelle in Brittainy, Tours in Gaul and other great monastic centers from which learning spread all over the land of the Gauls, the Franks, the Merovingians, the Carolingians, and the Teutons. There were saintly Christian kings and queens of this period, especially in Scotland and England, who encouraged and worked with their great monastic advisors, St. Columba, St. Augustine, St. Ninian, St. Dunstan, St. Cuthbert, St. Gall. This was the age of the wonder and mystery of the Church Alive in the farthest corners of the then known world. How mysterious and wonderful that it should have been founded first by the Christian witnesses who settled in England and Ireland, then Scotland, from 40 A.D. to 1200 A.D., permeating the Roman Empire and far beyond it and receiving accordingly all the classic learning, the good roads, the well-built towns and small cities which the Roman Empire had such a genius for establishing.

When the Roman legions withdrew, by God's mercy the most gifted sons and daughters of the kings of the tribes of Ireland, Scotland and England were led into the monastic life, and we have the thrilling story of the extraordinary activities of St. Patrick and St. Brigid and St. Columba. These people were austere ascetics filled with glorious love for their Lord Jesus Christ, who engaged in constant prayer and fasting and self-denial; they also studied, illumined the whole Bible, farmed and raised livestock, and walked and witnessed to everyone they met in Britannia, Gaul, Brittany Iberia and Germania. They healed the sick, comforted the sorrowing, preached the good news of Jesus and His resurrection and established hundreds of little monasteries and schools where learning and beauty and art were kept alive in what are known as the Dark Ages. As a matter of fact, the Dark Ages weren't very dark at all because of the extraordinarily creative activities of these men and women. The Church was alive, leading its hungry, needy, pagan listeners out of the arid worship of gods, goddesses, wood and stone to the feet of a personal savior.

And then through the Middle Ages, "the Age of Faith," when the great monasteries flourished and even kings learned the power of confession and penance and prayer, through the Reformation when there took place a great resurgence of the liberty in faith and life and Bible study and prayer which the early Christians knew, through the so-called "Age of Reason" when the mind and the pride of knowledge and discovery ruled, down to the present time, when it's being rediscovered that the heart and soul must balance this pride of mind and we must once again learn from the great contemplatives, the great lovers (like St. Francis), the great "interceders," the great witnesses of past centuries.

Perhaps two modern examples illustrate best of all the mystery and the wonder of the Church Alive. We in America who feel committed to the institution of the Church and the ongoing order and security of it, have trouble comprehending the extraordinarily courageous and creative ways in which it has been established in third world nations. I am thinking of a story that I heard in Korea when I visited there several years ago. The story has it that in the 1860's an American gun boat penetrated the sea of Japan and sailed up to the Han River in Korea to the outskirts of the former Imperial City, Seoul. Korea was then called the Hermit Kingdom because it was so deliberately cut off from the outside world by its emperors. The gun boat came right into the river where it was attacked and destroyed by the soldiers of the Korean emperor because of his fear of foreign invasion. On the gun boat was a young American missionary who was carrying into Korea a Bible which had been translated by a Chinese Christian into Korean. This young missionary was captured when the gun boat was destroyed, and the soldiers of the emperor shot him on the beach. Before he was shot, he handed his Bible to the sergeant in charge of the Korean soldiers. The sergeant thrust it into his tunic before he proceeded to the execution and that evening when he was preparing for bed he felt it there. He pulled it out and, as this particular Korean could read Chinese script, he read it through and was so taken with it that he papered the walls of his little hut with the pages of this Bible. Daily he would read different passages until he himself was converted to Christ and began witnessing to other Koreans. This was a tiny and feeble beginning. Earlier some Chinese Christians who had been converted to Christianity in China, members of the Royal Court of the Chinese emperor, came to Korea and witnessed to Korean noblemen and women. There was quite a flourishing community of Christians in the early 1800's in Korea until the emperor got wind of it and saw to it that all of them were martyred.

Fifty years later one single martyred Protestant missionary handed a Bible to his executioner and a tragic and violent event took place in the emperor's own palace. In a palace coup, the crown prince was seriously wounded. The emperor was in despair. None of his oriental doctors could heal the crown prince. The emperor heard that there was an American doctor who wanted to come into Korea from Japan to share his skills as well as his faith. He sent for this doctor, and the doctor came. The emperor said to him, "Can you heal my son? For if you can I will give you anything for which you ask." The doctor replied, "Yes, I can heal your son, but please open your country to other religions besides the Buddhist, Confucian and Animist religions and allow us Christians to come in and tell your people of our Lord Jesus Christ."

Here is indeed a mystery: why Korea during that particular

century? God must have worked in the mind and heart of the emperor to overcome his suspicion; God must have used the need of the emperor's son to open a door; and God must have heard the prayers of hundreds of Americans and American churches that this door be opened. And so the Christian Church was born in Korea through two modern saints— a Presbyterian missionary and a doctor. The prayer has continued; every morning between 6 and 7 A.M. hundreds of thousands of Koreans gather for prayer in both their small and large churches throughout South Korea and this mighty force has carried them literally through oppression, invasion and war until, when Billy Graham visited Korea in 1974, 1,500,000 Koreans gathered in Seoul to hear him.

One of the most mysterious and wonderful answers to prayer that has come to us is the story of how Christ through David Livingstone opened Africa to Christ, one man on his knees who felt a call and got up off his knees to obey it.

Livingstone was among the first to open up the "Dark Continent" of Africa to the light of the Gospel. Then, for several years, no word was heard of him. The reporter, Henry M. Stanley, set out to find him. It would be like finding a needle in a haystack.

Stanley comments on his progress, "My sicknesses were frequent, and, during my first attack of African fever, I took up my Bible to while away the tedious, feverish hours in bed. Though incapacitated from the march, my temperature being constantly at 105° Fahr., it didn't prevent me from reading, when not light-headed."

After his recovery he reports:

"I flung myself on my knees, and poured out my soul utterly in secret prayer to Him who had led me here *mysteriously* into Africa, there to reveal Himself, and His will. I became then inspired with fresh desire to serve Him to the utmost.

"My mission to find Livingstone was very simple, and

was a clear and definite aim. All I had to do was to free my mind from all else, and relieve it of every earthly desire but the finding of the man whom I was to seek. It produced a delightful tranquility which was foreign to me while in Europe.

"At last I heard of a white man at Ujiji on Lake Tanganyika. After many dangers, I managed to arrive there and met a white man who appeared to me that he could be no other than Livingstone. I said to this man, doffing my helmet and bowing, 'Dr. Livingstone, I presume.' Smiling cordially, Dr. Livingstone lifted his cap and answered briefly, 'Yes.' I then said, 'I thank God, Doctor, that I have been permitted to see you.' "

After this, Livingstone and Stanley spent months together at Ujiji in daily prayer and Bible study. Livingstone once confided to Stanley, "Christ was the beginner of the Christianity that has now spread over a large part of the world; then came the twelve apostles. I feel sometimes as if I was a beginner for attacking Central Africa, and that others will shortly come; after those, there will come the thousand workers you speak of. The whole earth shall be filled with the knowledge of the Lord, as the water covers the sea." When they parted, Stanley knew that God had appointed him to return to Africa to help complete the work of Livingstone.

It happened as Livingstone foresaw it. Wave after wave of missionaries came to Africa. Some were martyred, others died of disease; but before they died, they established a growing Church.

And now, a hundred years later, a mighty example of the force of prayer and witness has just hit the world news stands from Uganda in Africa. We have all been reading a great deal about the anguishing arrests, tortures and martyrdom of Christians that have been taking place there under the tyrant Idi Amin. The gripping firsthand story of the Rt. Rev. Festo Kivengere who with his wife escaped from Uganda after the murder of the Archbishop Janani Luwum has just been sent to me. Bishop Kivengere has been the Anglican Bishop of the Diocese of Kigesi since 1972. This diocese, smaller in land area than the state of New Hampshire, had some 30,000 confirmations in 1976, more than the entire Episcopal Church in the United States. The Bishop is also the leader of the East African team of the Africa Enterprise Organization and is one of the members of the central committee of the Billy Graham World Evangelization Program. This is what the bishop tells us of the martyrdom of the Christian Church in Uganda:

I love Idi Amin. I have never been his enemy. I wish somebody would take that message back to him. If I were in Uganda, I would shout it from the house-tops. If I could get near President Amin, I would tell him to his face. Actually, he knows it already.

Is it surprising that I love him? It shouldn't be. This is a purely Christian response to the tragic events of recent weeks.

His grace, Archbishop Luwum, gave us the passage in Mark 6:45–51 four days before he died. We bishops were sitting there discussing the arrest of one bishop and the midnight search at gunpoint of the archbishop's house. Luwum was full of peace and courage. He said, "My wife, Mary, and I have been deeply blessed this morning by reading in Mark 6." As he read, we saw the Lord Jesus on the mountain alone watching the disciples in a storm at sea making headway painfully in rowing. "For the last four days," said Janani, "the Lord has seen us in this council making headway painfully. But I see the road ahead very clearly." What road? The road across the stormy seas of Uganda.

Recently we have been caught in high waves and the winds coming contrary. The bishops and the archbishop were accused of having something to do with arms to overthrow the government, which was a complete falsehood. We don't believe in arms, they have never solved any problem. They create wounds which they never heal. We believe in the creative love of the Lord Jesus, and our Church will not be victimized by hatred. Luwum stood for this, and so did I.

But we speak the truth in love against injustices, against brutalities, against dehumanizing elements that intimidate a community. On January 30th I spoke against the evils of the misuse of authority before 30,000 people including intelligence officers, policemen, military, governors and all. Together with Luwum, we Bishops were trying at that time to present a document to President Amin expressing our position.

Do not think that when the weather is rough, the waves are beating on the boat, the winds are contrary, and Christians seem to be standing in a helpless situation, *that faith is not there nor joy in the Lord. These can be deeper when the weather becomes rough.*

Then, "after midnight" . . . there are times in our lives when it is after midnight. For us, the 16th and 17th of February were past midnight, *but He came! Bless Him, He always comes.* Our archbishop went to his arrest straight as an arrow, strengthened by the grace of Jesus. Afterwards we knew that he had died at the hands of violent men who had become enemies because the truth hurt them.

Jesus came to his disciples walking on top of the waves. Some of us would prefer to report that He always first removes the storm, the waves subside and then He comes. But, no, He walked to them on the crest of the wild waves. Then He spoke. He is speaking in Uganda today. True, there is real havoc, as there always is when rulers feel threatened and desperate. Hundreds and thousands of citizens are being got rid of. But one dear lady said to a bishop on February 19th: "Praise God! This experience has pushed us fifty times forward!" Jesus has brought peace and praise. Even though we could not get the body of our archbishop, there were 4,500 people in the Kampala cathedral on February 20th. After the service, they stood around the grave where he would have laid, near Bishop Hannington, the first martyr of the Uganda Church, and they sang praises to God. It was a melting time.

I was not there. On Saturday it became very clear that I was the next to be taken. This is the third time that I have been reported dead, so I am beginning to taste the meaning of resurrection!

So on the very 19th and 20th when *you in the West were praying for us* because of the news report of my arrest, we didn't sleep. We were trying to escape all that night—getting lost in the mountains. And poor Mera, she was suffering from bronchitis and tonsilitis as we climbed on foot, treking through the mountains in the dark night, led by a lovely Christian young man who knew the country well.

We made it, because Jesus was with us! We had been slowly climbing for two and a half hours till we reached the top. At 6:30 in the morning—I'll never forget the experience—the young man said, "now you are across the border, you can breathe a little freer!" We each sat down on a stone, wet with the dew and rather exhausted, and we praised Jesus. We knew that His people were praying for us and we had made our escape.

Please don't stop praying. Pray for the bishops who are still in Uganda and pray for the Church, that in the storm they may continue to see Jesus walking to them on top of the waves. I hope you are praying for President Amin realistically. I love him because Jesus tells me to. *I believe in a change that is going to bring reconciliation to Uganda, remove the elements of destruction and bring a beautiful reconstruction.*

The Church which started on Calvary is going to survive. It is the Church of the resurrected Savior, and the gates of hell can never overcome it. Whether I am in Uganda or not, my duty remains the same. As long as He gives me breath, I am going to shout: *"Behold! Behold the Lamb!"* That is what my archbishop *died doing. That is what the bishops who are still in the country— thirteen of them—are doing.*

May you, too, behold Him coming to you over the waves, hear His voice, and commit your life to Him.

And so it goes century after century, everywhere, a few handfuls of people have gone to spread the word, the Good News, and the tiny Church has been established—it has grown and grown and grown in spite of its virtual destruction in many areas of the world. It may have died out in one place only to spring up in another, but it has grown as Jesus said it would when he promised us, "If you have faith as a grain of mustard seed you shall say unto this mountain, be thou taken up and cast into the midst of the sea and this shall be done unto you according to your faith."

I have been fascinated in reading from the Gallup Polls recently about the growing vitality of our Christian faith in this country. Not only in the mainline churches, but in the many Christian ministries that are springing up within the mainline churches. I was particularly struck in reading in an issue of *U.S. News and World Report* (April 11, 1977) which gave statistics where the Church is most alive and most growing in this nation as of this time, and then quoted a famous sociologist, Dr. Arthur Berger, who tells us that he sees every sign of a great religious awakening beginning to take place in this country. Isn't it wonderful that whenever the Church seems to be dying down and becoming strait-jacketed in rigid formulas, rules, regulations, institutional bureaucracy and apathy, Christ mysteriously raises up some flaming spirits, whom he injects into his body as a doctor injects a blood transfusion into a sick body and that body gets well and lives on.

Running through it all has been the mysterious power of living, persistent, passionate prayer, because a few have been inspired to care so deeply that they have taken Jesus at His word, when he said to his disciples, "Pray without ceasing."

"This is my body which is given for you:
this do in remembrance of me.
This cup is the new testament in my blood,
which is shed for you."

LUKE 22:19–20

"That we may evermore dwell in Him and
He in us."

PRAYER OF HUMBLE ACCESS,
SERVICE OF HOLY COMMUNION,
BOOK OF COMMON PRAYER

18 ✣ THE MYSTERY OF HOLY COMMUNION

WHETHER we think of the Holy Eucharist (which means thanksgiving) as a memorial of Jesus giving His body and blood in our behalf, or think of it as the sharing of His real presence with us as we partake of the bread and wine, or believe that He actually in His total person is present as we eat His body and drink His blood, the mystery of His total self-offering for us and the mystery of our Holy Communion with Him in response to this self-offering remains the means of grace and the hope of glory for His millions of faithful people throughout the world. The binding and empowering mystery and reminder of His continuing presence with us is abundantly and tinglingly symbolized every time we participate in this His body and blood. The great Communion Hymn describes it:

> Here, O my Lord, I see thee face to face:
>   Here would I touch and handle things unseen;
> Here grasp with firmer hand eternal grace,
>   And all my weariness upon thee lean.
>
> Here would I feed upon the Bread of God;
>   Here drink with thee the royal Wine of heaven;
> Here would I lay aside each earthly load,
>   Here taste afresh the calm of sin forgiven.
>
> I have no help but thine; nor do I need
>   Another arm save thine to lean upon;
> It is enough, my Lord, enough indeed;
>   My strength is in thy might, thy might alone.
>
> Mine is the sin, but thine the righteousness,
>   Mine is the guilt, but thine the cleansing Blood,
> Here is my robe, my refuge, and my peace;
>   Thy Blood, thy righteousness, O Lord, my God.*

Last year in New York, Bishop Festo Kivengere, the African Anglican Bishop of Uganda who has just escaped with his life from the wrath of Idi Amin, Bishop William Cox, Suffragan Bishop of the Diocese of Maryland, two laywomen (Mrs. Polly Wiley and myself), and a Presbyterian minister (the Reverend Clinton Glenn) and his wife lunched together and shared their hearts with one another. At the end of this occasion, Mr. Glenn said to us: ''I would like to suggest to you Episcopalians that I believe as we sat at this luncheon table and shared our deepest experiences with one another and have eaten with each other, that we have engaged in a sacrament.'' He was so right—there was no rank here, no

*William Bright, Hymn 208, *Protestant Episcopal Hymn Book.*

lay-clergy self-consciousness, no male-female tension—we were truly one in Christ. And so it is always when committed Christians engage together in dialogue and prayer. Bishop Kivengere had been sharing with us the enormous dangers he was experiencing as a Christian bishop in his own country, comforting his people who were being falsely accused and imprisoned, praying with those about to be executed, and confronting Idi Amin with his atrocities. We took hands around that table in that public restaurant in New York and prayed for one another, and we are still praying for one another.

Last year our Diocesan Committee on Evangelism went to a Roman Catholic convent in our area so that each of us might share with the other our own deepest experience of our Lord, and then affirm each other in the gifts that God had given each of us to use to His glory. We came as a committee; we went away after thirty-six hours as a family, His family. We had shared our deepest experience of Him with one another; we had realized both our individual personhood and our interrelation in Him; and we participated together in His body and blood so that when we left we felt that He was truly with us and in us. I covet this experience for every church committee.

The early Christians met this way informally, in catacombs, in houses, in caves, and shared their experiences with each other in just such deep and meaningful ways. There were no committees in those days. Organization yes, but not committees and commissions and task forces and panels. Their business was carried out in informal fellowship meetings and concluded with the Lord's supper.

One of the great experiences of my life was to be present at the final service of Holy Communion in the great hall of the Beaulieu Palace in Lausanne, Switzerland, in 1974, at the World Congress on Evangelization, where 4,000 conveners, delegates, and observers from around the world—

Greek Christians, Korean Christians, Chinese and Japanese Christians, Indonesian Christians, Christians from Russia, Europe, Africa, South America, Cuba, and the islands of the sea—together received His body and blood, and I, as a convener, a lay member of the Episcopal Church, U.S.A., helped for the first time in my life to pass the body and blood of Christ to that vast congregation, walking between a famous Presbyterian missionary from South Korea and an Anglican bishop.

On a huge screen on the stage before the eyes of the participants was flashed the picture of a loaf baked by an African Christian woman, and beside it a chalice fashioned from clay by an Indian Christian woman, and then we were shown the Holy Communion celebrations taking place around the world on remote coral islands in the South Pacific, forest clearings in Africa, small palm-thatched churches in India and South America, and mighty cathedrals and churches everywhere.

The recently martyred Archbishop Luwum of East Africa, with Bishop Kivengere of Kigezi in Uganda, Billy Graham, a distinguished Presbyterian preacher from Scotland, and several others, blessed the elements on the altar and then the consecrated bread and wine was passed down to us, the international conveners, who in turn passed it to that huge congregation while the great hymns of the Christian Church throughout the world were played and sung quietly as we all participated together—the body of Christ gathered from all the earth eating His body and drinking His blood at one place at one time, and then scattering to the far corners of the earth to bear witness to His risen power and presence. After the service the twenty-five African bishops present met with me and my friend, Polly Wiley, under the great "Time Clock" in the foyer ticking, ticking, inexorably and exactly the number of new souls being born into the world every minute, every hour, every day, God's new created beings to whom

He was sending *us* to love and to serve and to bring to His feet. We stood, the African bishops and ourselves, with our arms about each other's shoulders and prayed aloud that our Lord, who had just shared with us His body and blood, would empower us to witness for Him wherever He called us to go. This we have tried to do since that stupendous experience of togetherness, and some of us have gone to our deaths because of that witness, some have been imprisoned, some have been tortured, some have been exiled, and some have loved and endured and shone in the face of all the difficulties and challenges with which life has confronted us on all the spiritual frontiers of the world, committed to one another as members of His blood kin. Isn't this the inner meaning? "Unless you eat my flesh and drink my blood, you have no life in you, for my flesh is food indeed and my blood is drink indeed."

In the summer of 1976, during the celebration in this country of the Bicentennial, the Roman Catholic Church called a great Eucharistic Congress in Philadelphia. To this congress, in preparation for the celebration of the Eucharist, Pope Paul VI sent a message which reads as follows:

To all of you in Philadelphia.

To you, Americans.

To you, men and women from all parts of the world, assembled for the International Eucharistic Congress.

It is the Bishop of Rome who speaks to you, the successor of the Apostle Peter, the Pope of the Catholic Church, the Vicar of Christ on earth.

He speaks to greet you, to assure you of his prayers, to have you hear in his voice the echo of Christ's words, and, thus—to some extent—to open up to you the deep meaning of the mystery that you are celebrating.

We ask you to be silent, to be silent now and try to listen within yourselves to an inner proclamation:

The Lord is saying: "Be assured, I am with you" (Matthew 28:20), "I am here," He is saying, "because this is My body! This is the cup of My blood!"

The mystery of His presence is thus enacted and celebrated: The mystery of His sacramental, but real and living presence. Jesus, the teacher of humanity, is here; He is calling for you (John 11:28).

Yes, He is calling you, each one by name! The mystery of the Eucharist is, above all, a personal mystery: Personal, because of His divine presence—the presence of Christ, the word of God made man; personal, because the Eucharist is meant for each of us; for this reason Christ has become living bread, and is multiplied in the sacrament, in order to be accessible to every human being who receives Him worthily, and who opens to Him the door of faith and love.

The Eucharist is a mystery of life! Christ says: "He who eats this bread shall live" (John 6:51).

The Eucharist is a mystery of suffering, yes; and a mystery of death! A mystery of redemptive passion; a mystery of sacrifice, consummated by Christ for our salvation. It is the mystery of the cross, reflected and commemorated in the sacrament which makes us share in the Lord's immolation, in order to associate us in His resurrection. Today, in this time, the Eucharist is the food for our earthly pilgrimage; tomorrow, in the life to come, it will be our everlasting happiness.

The Eucharist is, therefore, a mystery of love. It makes all of us who eat the same bread into a single body (I Corinthians 10:17), living by means of one spirit. It makes us one family: brothers and sisters united in solidarity with one another (Ephesians 4:16), and all of us dedicated to giving witness, in mutual love, to the fact that we really are the followers of Christ (John 13:35).

May it always be this way, beloved, brethren, and sons and daughters!

With our apostolic blessing: in the name of the Father, and of the Son, and of the Holy Spirit, Amen!

In conclusion I say for all of you who read this book a beautiful prayer that was sent to me by a friend which expresses the mystery of the Eucharist in words better than I can do.

THE PRAYER OF THE CHALICE

Father, to Thee I raise my whole being
—a vessel emptied of self. Accept,
Lord, this my emptiness, and so fill
me with Thyself—Thy light, Thy
love, Thy Life—that these Thy
precious gifts may radiate
through me and overflow the
chalice of my heart into the
hearts of all with whom I
come in contact this day
revealing unto them
the beauty of
Thy joy
and
wholeness
and
the
serenity
of Thy peace
which nothing can destroy.

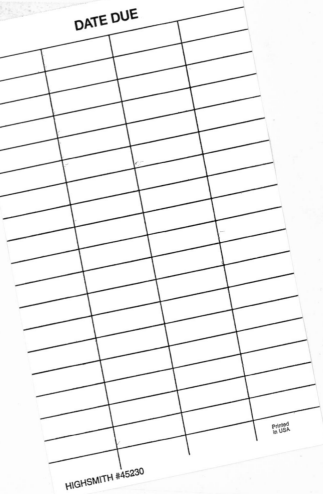

DATE DUE

Printed
in USA

HIGHSMITH #45230